HORSE MOVEMENT
Structure, Function and
Rehabilitation

HORSE MOVEMENT

Structure, Function and Rehabilitation

Gail Williams BA (Hons) VPhys, PhD, MASSVAP, MIAVRPT

Illustrated by Alexa McKenna BVM&S

J. A. ALLEN

First published in 2014 by J.A. Allen, an imprint of
The Crowood Press Ltd, Ramsbury, Marlborough Wiltshire SN8 2HR

enquiries@crowood.com

www.crowood.com

This impression 2021

British Library Cataloguing-in-Publication Data
A catalogue record for this book is available from the British Library.

ISBN 978 1 908809 11 7

Edited by Jane Lake

Designed and typeset by Paul Saunders

Printed and bound in India by Parksons Graphics Pvt. Ltd., Mumbai.

Contents

Useful websites

Gail Williams; www.gailwilliams.co.uk

Gail Williams Facebook page; www.facebook.com/Dr.Gail.Williams

ASSVAP (Association for the Scientific Study of Veterinary and Animal Physiotherapy); www.assvap.com

ASSVAP Facebook page; www.facebook.com/pages/assvap/244625052256925

ACE bandages can be obtained from ASSVAP (website as above)

International Symposium in Animal Musculoskeletal Practice (ISAMP); www.isamp.org

Publisher's note

The carpus in the forelimb corresponds to the wrist in the human but is commonly, although incorrectly, called the 'knee'. In this book we have bowed to common usage and called this joint the knee. The horse's true knee is located in the hind limb.

Acknowledgments

We would like to say thank you to all the following for their invaluable contribution to this book.

Bates Saddles Australia; www.batessaddles.com

Centaur Biomechanics; www.centaurbiomechanics.co.uk

Equine Articulated Skeletons (Walter Varco); www.equineskeletons.com

Fairfax Saddles; www.fairfaxsaddles.co.uk

Hannah Ray for the photo of Sarah Stretton, bottom of page 85; www.photographybyhr.co.uk

Helen Morrell of Surrey Vet Physio; www.surreyvetphysio.com

Kerry Millership of Friary Stables; www.friarystables.com

Marc Moggridge; www.burghleyimages.photoshelter.com

Naomi and Amber Franklin of Lazy Acres Event Team; www.lazyacresstables.co.uk

Nico Morgan for the photos of hind limb retraction on page 95 and the elite jumping horse on page 110; www.nicomorgan.com

Quintic Gait Analysis; www.quintic.com

Rebel Saddles; www.rebelsofsweden.co.uk

Sam Pawley Photography; www.photoboxgallery.com/sampawleyphotography

Sarah Stretton of Stretton Eventing; www.sarahstrettoneventing.co.uk

Foreword by Hilary M. Clayton

BVMS, PhD, Dipl ACVSMR, MRCVS
Professor and Mary Anne McPhail Dressage Chair Emerita
President Sport Horse Science, LC

As I meandered through the pages of this book, the wisdom of the proverb 'an ounce of prevention is worth a pound of cure' came to mind. The basic premise upon which the book is written is that many unsoundness issues of horses have an insidious onset involving a developmental stage when signs indicative of an impending problem can be recognised if the observer knows what to look for. Therefore, early recognition and appropriate therapy may avoid progression to an overt lameness or performance issue. The reader learns how to detect and interpret subtle, and not so subtle, changes in the horse's posture and demeanor that may be a forewarning of a developing problem. An attractive feature of this book is that it's punctuated throughout by interesting examples to illustrate the relevance of the factual information.

As prey animals, horses are adept at hiding the signs of pain from their predators but, if you learn what to look for, it is possible to detect many problems that lie in the grey area between soundness and lameness. The authors draw our attention to the importance of static (standing) and dynamic (locomotor) posture as valuable indicators of musculoskeletal pain or dysfunction that have, perhaps, not received sufficient emphasis in the past. Early identification of postural problems allows early treatment which can often prevent the progression of a minor injury into a full blown lameness problem.

Having been a teacher of veterinary anatomy for many years, I appreciated the functional anatomical approach; knowledge of muscle structure and function is the cornerstone upon which to build an understanding of equine movement and athletic performance. The text is enhanced by clear and beautifully drawn illustrations that are the work of the second author, veterinary surgeon Alexa McKenna. It is particularly informative to see the muscles displayed individually which facilitates the reader's appreciation of each muscle's attachments and actions. In addition, an ample number of good photographs illustrate various aspects of equine performance and performance evaluation techniques, including thermal images, pressure mapping and motion analysis.

Topical areas in research and practice, such as saddle fitting and hoof care, each occupy a full chapter and rightly so since these are two of the most important aspects of management to be addressed in caring for an athletic horse. As in other sections of the book, the reader is guided through the relevant anatomy and the chain of events that is set in motion by back pain or foot pain. It then becomes obvious why signs of dysfunction are often manifest in a different part of the body than the initiating cause.

Preventive and rehabilitative care are addressed by the use of passive and dynamic stretches and proprioceptive awareness techniques. The latter are used extensively in human physiotherapy, especially during athletic training and performance, and there is growing enthusiasm for their use in horses. The potential value of equine proprioceptive techniques lies in improving the horse's awareness of body position and movements and in enhancing muscular activation and coordination, which are highly relevant both to athletic performance and to rehabilitation.

Congratulations to the authors for compiling a book that is both interesting to read and relevant to current training practices. The information herein will be useful for analysing, interpreting and improving the performance of our equine athletes.

April 2014

CHAPTER ONE

An Introduction to Functional Anatomy

Structure. Function. Two completely ordinary, simple, everyday words. But when you are able to apply them to the way a horse moves, it will take you to a level of understanding that will empower you to increase his performance, resilience to injury and provide him with a pain free, active life.

Posture

A single word can indeed be substituted for structure and function: posture. But now you are probably thinking 'What has my horse's posture got to do with anything?' The answer is that it has everything to do with the way he stands, moves and performs. But even more importantly poor posture is significantly implicated in primary injury and secondary dysfunction in the horse.

For the horse, sound and lame are two ends of a very wide spectrum and, in the absence of trauma, a series of small compensatory postural changes can take place over several days, weeks or even months. By the time that clinical lameness manifests, a number of small, sub-clinical anatomical pressures have been created. Without an appreciation of this phenomenon, treatment of the primary lameness, whilst ignoring the compensatory changes that led to it, will simply lead to a relapsing or evolving condition. Further, in the absence of physical trauma, escalating subtle postural compensations can eventually result in lameness in anatomical structures far away from the original source of pain.

Why should this be so? The answer lies in the fact that the horse evolved primarily as a prey animal. His major means of defence is to outrun a predator. Therefore, the predator will select as its target that which it perceives as the sick, lame or lazy animal from the herd. Consequently it is in the interests of the horse to disguise that he is in any way impaired from running because of pain. Horses, more so than any other animal, have developed strategies to conceal injury, and therefore by the time that lameness is expressed, the animal is already in significant pain and may have been so for some time. Further if postural compensations have been longstanding, he may be experiencing pain in many areas of his body and the particular lameness that he is exhibiting may be completely disassociated with the original painful area. So if only the presenting lameness is addressed, the mechanisms which created that lameness are still likely to be present.

It takes a very experienced and critical eye to perceive pre-lameness postural compensations in the horse. It is what veterinary surgeons will refer to as a sub-clinical lameness, as there is dysfunctional movement but nothing that would classify it as clinically 'lame'. New advances in gait analysis with horses have shown the remarkable extent by which the horse can imperceptibly transfer his body weight to compensate for pain. An original postural compensation can result in a minor overload of another anatomical structure, which in turn becomes painful and the horse must shift his weight again and again. This leads to a downward spiral of complex compensatory mechanisms which inexorably result in observable lameness when the horse is unable to disguise his pain further.

Functional anatomy

The basis of this book is functional anatomy, which is an important scientific discipline. Not only is it necessary for an understanding of the correct movement of the horse, but it is vitally important to understand the anatomical pressures associated with riding, competition, training, over-training, injury, disease and rehabilitation. There are welfare implications to also consider, not just for the leisure horse but particularly in the sport horse. Injury is an unfortunate effect of sporting life and brings with it pain, and incapacity. For the owner it also brings the inevitable emotional and economic costs. It is a sad fact that 70 per cent of horses involved in sport will sustain at least one lame episode in each competitive season. Some of these will, of course, be as a result of direct trauma such as a fall, striking a solid fence etc., but many of them will be as a result of compensatory gait patterns which have gone unnoticed by the rider/trainer/owner. How many times has the veterinary surgeon or veterinary physiotherapist heard the plaintive cry of 'He was fine when I rode him yesterday, but he's come out of the stable lame today'?

The other possible scenario which is frequently encountered by the vet or physiotherapist is the horse that has developed the so-called 'poor performance syndrome', i.e. he is no longer able to undertake a movement that he has been able to do previously, such as refusing jumps, he shows an inability to perform lateral movements one way or another, or his temperament has changed in some way. Very often the history given by the rider will be of their horse apparently 'resisting' or 'refusing to go forwards'. Whatever the history, the primary factor is one in which the horse is not doing what is wanted of him. Unfortunately some riders and trainers will not even consider pain as a possible cause for temperament changes or athletic resistance, and will use strong aids such as the use of a whip or spurs to 'overcome' *his* problems. The word 'his' has been emphasised because it is automatically assumed by these riders/trainers that the problem is with the horse.

However, if you learn anything from this book at all, in the interests of equine welfare make it the following.

If a horse is not doing what you want him to do there are usually three main causes:

1. He doesn't understand what you want him to do.

2. He is not physically capable of doing what you want him to do.

3. It hurts him to do what you want him to do.

And guess what? *None* of those are his fault, so before you start aggressively using your whip or spurs, make sure that you have ruled those three factors out.

By the time you have read this book, you will be in a much better position to assess your horse physically and functionally, and you will be equipped with a number of skills to help your horse become the very best that he can possibly be. Not only that, you will be able to identify and resolve any physical or functional problems before they result in significant pain and lameness. Nonetheless it is emphasised that the information given here is not a substitute for direct professional involvement from your vet or from a fully qualified veterinary physiotherapist such as a member of ASSVAP (Association for the Scientific Study of Veterinary and Animal Physiotherapy). If in any doubt at all, you should consult one of these professionals.

What is functional anatomy?

Functional anatomy is essentially the study of movement and physical activity. Whilst the latter is basically a physiological subject, physiology and anatomy are close bedfellows and cannot be easily separated. However, functional anatomy is the fundamental building block of biomechanics and is therefore generally considered to be a mechanical system. Therefore, as a visual science, the unaided eye is used to examine the structure and movement of the equine body. Also palpation (using the senses of touch and pressure) skills are utilised to provide further information beyond surface visualisation. For the animal healthcare professional, particularly vets and veterinary physiotherapists, eyes and hands are their most important tools. Eyes can appreciate the surface anatomy, both static and dynamic, whilst palpation can provide an appreciation of the condition and mass of deeper anatomical structures. Effectively hands are used as substitute eyes to add information from the deeper anatomy that cannot be viewed to the information gleaned from the surface visualisation.

Horses are vertebrate animals, which means they have a vertebral column (axial skeleton) attached to which are limbs (appendicular skeleton). Bones are usually joined together by means of arthroses (joints). Muscles are attached to bone by way of tendons. Muscles contract and relax and transmit the forces they generate via the tendons to the bones, to either change joint angles to produce locomotion, or to stabilise joints when stationary, enabling standing. In basic biomechanical terms we can think of joints, particularly in the appendicular skeleton, as levers. As in all mechanics theory, the more efficient the levers, the greater the power produced and the more effective the movement generated.

In the equine body, if the levers are malfunctioning because of musculoskeletal pain, then the static and dynamic posture of the horse is altered, and the smooth operation of the whole system is impaired. As outlined earlier in this chapter, this may not be immediately evident to the rider/trainer. It can be a long road from sound to lame. Sound and lame are the black and white of the situation, in the absence of trauma it can be a very long journey between the two, with movement compensations being piled on top of each other. To begin to appreciate how important static and dynamic posture is in the horse, we must start to think not in terms of sound and lame, but in terms of functional and dysfunctional movement.

The majority of injuries leading to pain and dysfunction have mechanical causes. Forces and force-related factors not only lead to injury but have an effect on its severity. We must therefore have a definition of 'injury'. Injury is the damage caused by physical trauma to musculoskeletal tissues. Such trauma may be sub-clinical and induce subtle postural adaptations, or it may be major and immediately give rise to observable injury. But these major traumas in themselves produce postural compensations.

For example, in quadrupeds, such as the horse, body weight is transferred away from an injured limb to its diagonal. Therefore if the left forelimb is painful, the horse will throw as much of his weight off that limb to the right hind limb, increasing the forces of locomotion to that diagonal limb. Imagine trotting this lame horse, his head will nod up and down. He will lift his head up high when the left forelimb is on the ground and throw his weight off that limb and back onto the right hind limb. When the right forelimb comes into stance phase, he drops his head low to prepare to throw

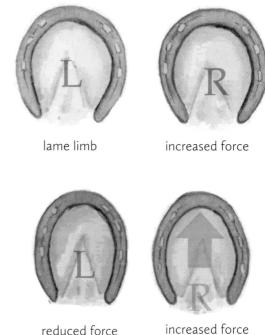

lame limb   increased force

reduced force   increased force

it up again when the painful left forelimb it put to the ground. By doing this he automatically transfers an abnormally high force off his left hind limb onto the right forelimb (Figure 1.1). Therefore *every* limb is experiencing a compensatory mechanism, not just the lame one.

This is a very simple explanation for what is, in its sub-clinical form, a complex process. It is purely to demonstrate how compensatory postural changes as a result of pain can affect the whole body in terms of forces on musculoskeletal tissues which may result in secondary pathology elsewhere in the body.

Figure 1.1 Illustration of transfer of weight in lame horse trotting. If the left fore is lame, the horse compensates by throwing his weight back onto the diagonal hind limb by lifting his head and neck.

Elastic energy in equine locomotion

Another important aspect of equine locomotion is the heavy reliance on elastic energy for forwards movement. As a prey animal, whose major means of defence is to outrun a predator, the horse has evolved to make greatest use of movements that do not require direct energy derived from food (ATP [adenosine triphosphate] derived from glycogen, fat, proteins etc.) which would drain energy levels on any activity that is not actually propelling the horse away from that predator. These movements are primarily those which involve movements of the limbs whilst they are non-weight bearing, such as flexion and protraction.

In physics **elasticity** is a physical property of materials which return to their original shape after they are deformed. When an elastic material is deformed due to an external force, it experiences internal forces that oppose the deformation and restore it to its original state if the external force is no longer applied. Put very simply, imagine an elastic band. If you stretch it you are applying an external force, but when you release it, it will return to its original length. So returning to its original length did not require any additional energy input, the elastic band simply stored the energy as part of the stretching process and released it to return the band to the original dimensions when you let it go.

All musculoskeletal tissues exhibit varying degrees of viscoelastic behaviour (i.e. time and rate dependent), but for the horse it is mainly the viscoelasticity of tendons in the distal (lower) limb, or tendinous tissue running through muscles that protract the fore and hind limb, that have highly evolved to display maximal elastic energy utilisation. In the biceps brachii, biomechanical studies have shown that the significant tendinous tissue that runs through the muscle from origin to insertion not only significantly contributes to the passive (lacking active energetic input) protraction of the forelimb, but increases the power over 100 times.

The major hind limb protractor is the iliopsoas, which has two parts – the iliacus and the psoas major. The iliacus origin covers the ventral surface of the ilium, whilst the psoas major origin arises along the ventral surfaces of the lumbar vertebrae transverse processes. They fuse to have a common insertion on the lesser trochanter on the medial aspect of the femur (Figure 1.2).

These muscles are primarily tendinous in structure so think of them as large straps of strong elastic. As the hip joint extends whilst the limb is on the floor undergoing retraction, these strong elastic bands stretch. As soon as the weight is taken off the hind limb, these elastic bands 'spring' back to bring the hip into flexion without any additional energetic input from vital energy stores and the rest of the hind limb follows passively.

In the distal limb the long tendons of the flexor muscles similarly store elastic energy as the limb is loaded and the fetlock extends towards the floor during weight bearing, and those tendons are stretched. As soon as the limb is lifted from the floor, the distal limb joints flex passively due to the release of elastic energy.

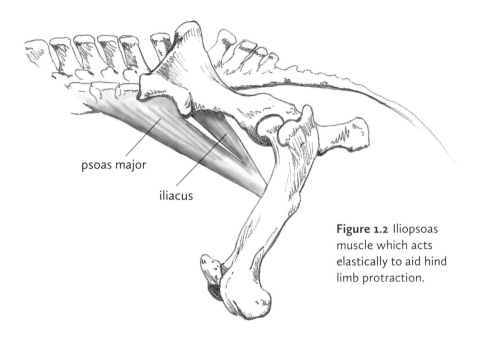

psoas major

iliacus

Figure 1.2 Iliopsoas muscle which acts elastically to aid hind limb protraction.

Watch a racehorse come out of a starting gate; his first movement is to drop the hindquarters to flex the hocks and stifles. The fore and hind toes are driven deep into the surface to create something akin to the effect of human athletes' starting blocks. For the first few strides, both his hind limbs move together in a bunny-hopping movement, with the toes digging into the surface until the elastic energy system can begin to function, at which time he will settle into the traditional transverse gallop. Until the elastic energy system begins to function he is in danger of stumbling and going down on his knees, or his hind feet can cut into the back of the front legs.

This elastic energy system is wonderful when the horse's dynamic posture is good. But if there is pain or muscular asymmetry or poor foot balance then it can become a liability. Also 'fine tuning' of this elastic energy system is provided by the antagonists, which are the muscle(s) acting in opposition to the muscle(s) providing the desired movement working eccentrically (lengthening whilst developing tension) whilst the elastic structures release energy. Pain in these antagonists can lead to erratic protraction or flexion of the limbs. For example, the main antagonist to the iliopsoas is the middle gluteal muscle. Pain in the gluteal muscle will lead to impaired retraction and decreased weight bearing in the affected hind limb. This in turn leads to inappropriate loading of the elastic structures required for efficient flexion and protraction of the limb. Similarly, changes in posture due to chronic, sub-clinical pain produce erratic behaviour in elastic structures resulting in less than optimal gait patterns.

Effects of forces on musculoskeletal tissues

These changes to the normal functioning of limb dynamics places abnormal stress and strain on other limb structures such as joints and ligaments. During normal, functional movement, all musculoskeletal tissues will acquire, via normal physiological responses, the mass and density required for the particular sporting/leisure requirements. Inappropriate loading leads to inappropriate physiological response leading to the potential for tissue damage which post-injury needs an intricate understanding of how to rehabilitate the horse to ensure a repair that will lead to the tissue recovering as much of its biomechanical function as possible.

Bone

Bone, particularly, is a remarkable adaptive tissue, and its response to stress and strain is to remodel very quickly, to lay down more bone tissue in areas of the skeleton that are experiencing the greatest loading challenges. This phenomenon was first described in the nineteenth century by Charles Darwin in his book *The Origin of Species* where he stated:

> With animals the increased use or disuse of parts has a marked influence; thus in the domestic duck the bones of the wing weigh less and the bones of the leg more, in proportion to the whole skeleton, than do the same bones in the wild duck; and this may be safely attributed to the domestic duck flying less and walking more than its wild parents.

Essentially, wild ducks fly more (and so have increased bone density in their wing bones) than domestic ducks that walk more (and so have increased density in their leg bones)

This observation found its way into the nineteenth century scientific literature in the form of 'Wolff's Law' which stated:

> Every change in the form and function of a bone or of their function alone is followed by certain definite changes in their internal architecture and equally definite secondary alterations in their external conformation, in accordance with mathematical laws.

Very simply this means that bone adapts to the stresses and strains put upon it by remodelling by reducing bone density in skeletal areas that are experiencing reduced loading, and increasing the bone density in skeletal areas that are experiencing increased loading.

Immobilisation leads to disuse osteoporosis in the bones that are immobilised. Post-injury, because of the body's immediate response to forces, recovery of bone density and strength can be made within weeks.

Ligaments and tendons

Ligaments, which generally serve to stabilise joints by joining bone to bone, and tendons, which attach the muscle to the bone, also respond to stress and strain and are very sensitive to training and disuse. Exercise leads not only to hypertrophy (increased diameter of fibres) but also an increase in strength. Normal exercise can increase ligament strength by over 20 per cent, whilst immobilisation can lead to a rapid deterioration in strength and stiffness as well as loss of important tissue constituents such as glycosaminoglycans. The site of the insertion of the tendon or ligament into the bone is particularly vulnerable, and whilst recovery of strength within the body of the ligament may only take weeks after immobilisation, the insertion site can take many months. Without a proper understanding of how tissues adapt to exercise and recover from injury, the insertion site can be stripped from the bone in an avulsion fracture, which is a particularly serious injury. An injury within the body of the ligament, if not rehabilitated satisfactorily, can lead to persistent joint instability, prolonged pain and progressive degeneration. Likewise tendon injury not rehabilitated appropriately will lead to significantly altered mechanics and will be prone to re-injury.

Ligaments also possess elastic qualities and contain special receptors known as mechanoreceptors which react when the ligament is stretched to the limit and the joint is near to its maximum movement and in danger of injury. They send 'help' signals to the surrounding muscles which react to act as dynamic stabilisers to protect the joint. Therefore ligaments are an important part of functional anatomy which, if loaded properly, can act as strong stabilisers protecting the joint from injury, but any impairment to loading due to postural changes or immobilisation leads to loss of strength and potentially permanent joint injury.

The tendons in the equine distal limb have a sophisticated and complex reaction to normal and abnormal forces which this book is not designed to address, but injury to these tendons can be some of the most devastating and economically significant injuries in equine sport. Healing is lengthy in time and requires highly skilled post-injury rehabilitation. We know that tendon failure can be the result of long-term postural compensation. Indeed in a retrospective study using force plates to study the forces generated by equine movement, scientists at Bristol Veterinary School demonstrated that changes in movement patterns could be detected up to two weeks prior to the actual injury.

Joints

Each joint has a range of motion (ROM) through which it normally operates and which determines the joint's mobility. ROM is joint specific and relative to individual conformation. Joints with more than one movement plane have a ROM for each plane.

The stability of the joint is directly related to its ROM because it is the ability of a joint to maintain an appropriate functional position throughout its range of motion. ROM is determined by the combined effects of the degree of bony fit, restraint provided by the joint capsule, ligaments and other periarticular surfaces, and the action of the muscles surrounding the joint. Injury to joints occurs when the joint exceeds its normal ROM, the tissues are violated and experience injury-producing forces.

The forces experienced by horses can be of considerable magnitude, especially in the speed or jumping horse, and injury-producing forces lead to tears in the menisci and/or articular cartilage degeneration. Of all types of connective tissue, articular cartilage (AC) is the most severely exposed to stress leading to wear and tear as it has a role in control of motion, transmission of load and maintenance of stability. It decreases the load by increasing the load-bearing surface because AC is plastic and capable of deformation.

During locomotion, the limb joints in the horse are constantly moving through their ROM. The short term effects of that movement are that the synovial fluid that lubricates the joint increases, which improves the nutrient supply to the AC and the removal of waste products. In the long term, with the application of appropriate forces and training within the joint's capacity the AC thickens, thus providing greater resistance to forces. Injury to the AC occurs (in the absence of fracture) due to overuse from excessive training, and repeated trauma causes a fracture of the cartilage matrix.

Fasciae

The final tissue that bears discussion in terms of functional anatomy is fasciae. Scientific investigation into this particular tissue is in its infancy, but research is now demonstrating that it has a marked role as a force transmitter in animal posture and movement regulation.

Fasciae are dense connective tissues that surround muscles, groups of muscles, blood vessels, nerves and internal organs. It binds some structures together whilst allowing others to slide smoothly over each other. The definition of fasciae was only finally determined in 2007 as 'All collagenous connective tissues whose morphology is dominantly shaped by tensional loading and which can be seen to be part of an interconnected tensional network throughout the whole body.'

The fascial body appears to be one large networking organ, with many bags and hundreds of rope-like local densifications, and thousands of pockets within pockets, all interconnected by sturdy septa as well as by looser connective tissue layers[1]. It extends uninterrupted from the head to the toes encapsulating all tissue structures and joint/organ capsules.

Under the microscope it is seen as numerous layers of collagen fibre bundles with each layer showing different orientations and separated by a thin layer of adipose tissue. They are typically punctured by nerve/artery/vein bundles which interestingly equate very well with traditional Chinese acupuncture points. Fasciae contract in a smooth muscle-like manner and influence musculoskeletal dynamics. However, the contractures of fasciae occur over a time frame of minutes to hours but can be strong enough to influence low-back stability and general biomechanics.

Fascial tissues are commonly utilised in dynamic energy storage for postural stability during movement. During movement, the supporting skeletal muscles contract more isometrically whilst the fascial elements lengthen and shorten like elastic springs, which clearly has a particular relevance to the horse because of his heavy reliance upon elastic energy for movement.

Proprioception

A very important factor in efficient static and dynamic posture is proprioception. Proprioception is the ability of an animal to know where his limbs/joints are in space and time without looking at them. For example, if you put your hand behind your back, you don't have to look to know where it is or what orientation your joints are in. Proprioception is such an important part of posture that is has been termed the sixth sense. We know that the fascial network serves as a sensory organ because it is densely innervated by myelinated sensory nerve endings including very specialist

---

1 Robert Schleip, Heike Jager, Werner Klingler. 'What is 'fascia'? A review of different nomenclatures.' *Journal of Bodywork & Movement Therapies* (2012) 16, 496–502

neural tissues such as Pacini corpuscles, Golgi tendon organs and Ruffini endings. In fact, the extent of the fascial system makes it the largest sensory organ in the body.

Its full biomechanical role, response to training and injury, however, are little understood at this time, but many physiotherapists have anecdotal evidence as to marked effect of fascial contraction on locomotion, and use myofascial release techniques as part of their treatment protocol.

The equine locomotor system is therefore a complex, multifactorial system in which not only do individual structures have individual effects, but they can also work in any number of combinations with other musculoskeletal structures. It is this individual and combined effect which produces movement. Injury or pain can have a profound effect on how these systems work and we must therefore take a journey through the functional anatomy of the horse to demonstrate these phenomena, and how to utilise this knowledge in your management, training and rehabilitation of the horse.

CHAPTER TWO

The Forelimb

In the next three chapters there are some of Alexa's brilliant illustrations to enable you to understand the anatomy of the horse and how it relates to function. Muscles have effects on joints and they can either move a joint through its range of movement (ROM) during locomotion, or stabilise a joint to facilitate standing. Very rarely does one muscle work alone and it will usually have 'synergists', which are other muscles that have a similar effect, and 'antagonists' which are muscles that have the opposite effect. For example, one muscle may flex a joint and another will extend the same joint. Although they both have an effect on the same joint their function is the opposite of the other.

During stance and unridden movement, the horse takes about 60 per cent of his weight on his front limbs. This is a general principle of veterinary mammalian movement in that the forelimbs are mainly for support of the trunk, whilst the hind limbs act to propel the animal forwards.

In this chapter we describe the major muscles of the forelimb and shoulder, giving their anatomical origins, insertions, innervation, function and any developmental problems associated with that particular muscle (or group of muscles).

We also describe what is known as the 'stay apparatus', which is the system by which the horse is able to sleep standing up.

Muscles of the shoulder

MEDIAL SHOULDER MUSCLES

TERES MAJOR (Figure 2.1)

ORIGIN Caudal border of scapula and subscapularis

INSERTION Teres tuberosity of humerus

INNERVATION Axillary nerve

FUNCTION Flexes shoulder

DEVELOPMENT ISSUES Shortness of stride

SUBSCAPULARIS (Figure 2.2)

ORIGIN Subscapular fossa of scapula

INSERTION Lesser tuberosity of humerus

INNERVATION Subscapular and axillary nerves

FUNCTION Extends shoulder

DEVELOPMENT ISSUES Tight restricted shoulder movement

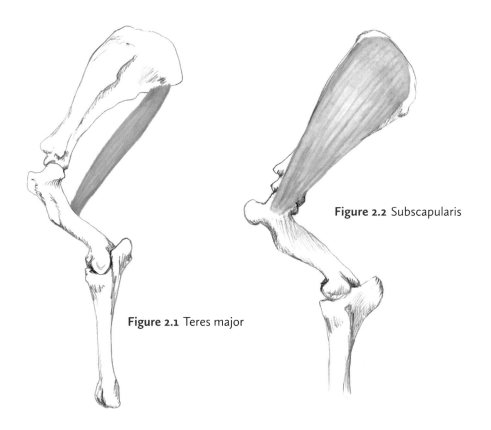

Figure 2.2 Subscapularis

Figure 2.1 Teres major

CORACOBRACHIALIS (Figure 2.3)

ORIGIN Coracoid process of scapula

INSERTION Proximomedial surface of humerus

INNERVATION Musculocutaneous nerve

FUNCTION Extends shoulder and adducts (brings towards) limb

DEVELOPMENT ISSUES Poor lateral work

BICEPS BRACHII (including lacertus fibrosus) (Figure 2.4)

ORIGIN Supraglenoid tubercle

INSERTION Radial tuberosity and medial collateral ligament; tendon of extensor carpi radialis via lacertus fibrosus

INNERVATION Musculocutaneous nerve

FUNCTION Extends shoulder, flexes elbow, forms part of stay apparatus

DEVELOPMENT ISSUES Effect mainly elastic but injury leads to lameness

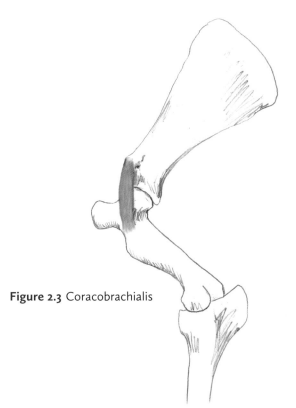

Figure 2.3 Coracobrachialis

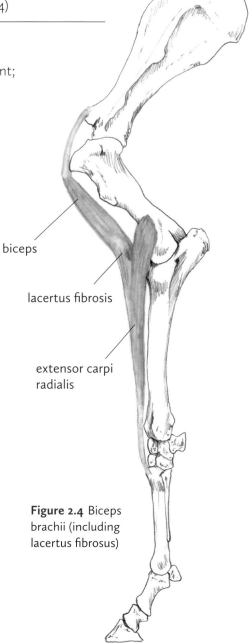

biceps

lacertus fibrosis

extensor carpi radialis

Figure 2.4 Biceps brachii (including lacertus fibrosus)

BRACHIALIS (Figure 2.5)

ORIGIN Proximocaudal surface of humerus

INSERTION Proximomedial surface of radius

INNERVATION Musculocutaneous nerve

FUNCTION Flexes elbow

DEVELOPMENT ISSUES Shortness of stride

TENSOR FASCIA ANTEBRACHII (Figure 2.6)

ORIGIN Caudal border of scapula and tendon of insertion of latissimus dorsi

INSERTION Olecranon and deep fascia of forearm

INNERVATION Radial nerve

FUNCTION Extends elbow joint

DEVELOPMENT ISSUES Shortness of stride in retraction

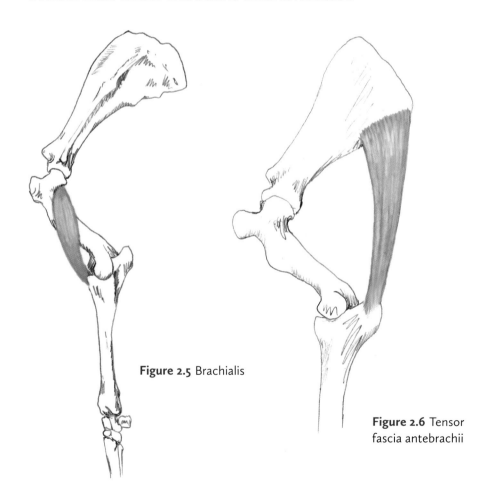

Figure 2.5 Brachialis

Figure 2.6 Tensor fascia antebrachii

LATERAL SHOULDER MUSCLES

DELTOIDEUS (Figure 2.7)

ORIGIN Scapular spine and caudal border of scapula

INSERTION Deltoid tuberosity of humerus

INNERVATION Axillary nerve

FUNCTION Flexes shoulder

DEVELOPMENT ISSUES Unlevelness and shortened stride in retraction

TERES MINOR (Figure 2.8)

ORIGIN Distal half of caudal border of scapula

INSERTION Proximal to deltoid tuberosity of humerus

INNERVATION Axillary nerve

FUNCTION Flexes shoulder

DEVELOPMENT ISSUES As above

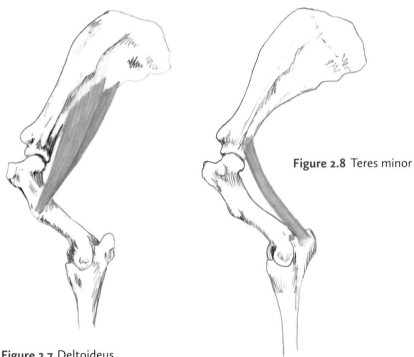

Figure 2.8 Teres minor

Figure 2.7 Deltoideus

SUPRASPINATUS (Figure 2.9)

ORIGIN Supraspinous fossa, scapular cartilage and spine

INSERTION Greater and lesser tubercles of humerus

INNERVATION Suprascapular nerve

FUNCTION Extends and stabilises shoulder; insertion acts as collateral ligament of shoulder

DEVELOPMENT ISSUES Instability of shoulder and potential subluxation of shoulder joint (sweeny)

INFRASPINATUS (Figure 2.10)

ORIGIN Infraspinatus fossa, scapular cartilage and spine

INSERTION Strong tendon distal to lateral insertion of supraspinatus muscle

INNERVATION Suprascapular nerve

FUNCTION Extends and stabilises shoulder

DEVELOPMENT ISSUES As above

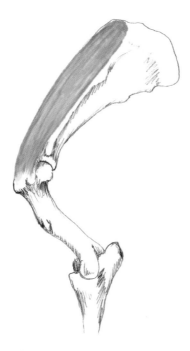

Figure 2.9 Supraspinatus

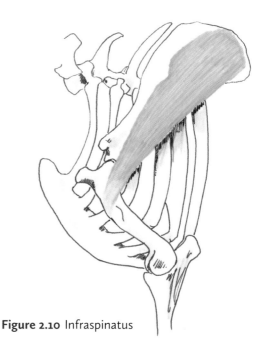

Figure 2.10 Infraspinatus

TRICEPS BRACHII

a. long head (Figure 2.11a)

ORIGIN Caudal border of scapula

INSERTION Tuber of olecranon

INNERVATION Radial nerve

FUNCTION Flexes and extends elbow

DEVELOPMENT ISSUES Shortness of stride, particularly in retraction

b. lateral head (Figure 2.11a)

ORIGIN Deltoid tuberosity of humerus

INSERTION Tuber of olecranon

INNERVATION Radial nerve

FUNCTION Extends elbow joint

DEVELOPMENT ISSUES As above

c. medial head (Figure 2.11b)

ORIGIN Medial surface of humerus

INSERTION Tuber of olecranon

INNERVATION Radial nerve

FUNCTION Extends elbow joint

DEVELOPMENT ISSUES As above

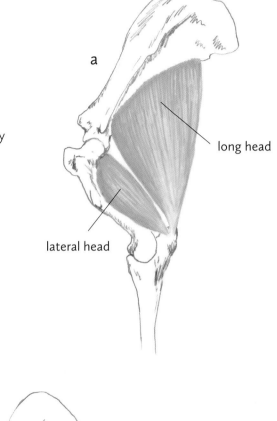

a

long head

lateral head

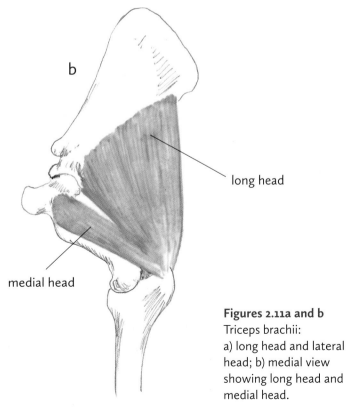

b

long head

medial head

Figures 2.11a and b
Triceps brachii:
a) long head and lateral head; b) medial view showing long head and medial head.

CAUDOMEDIAL FOREARM

SUPERFICIAL DIGITAL FLEXOR (Figure 2.12)

ORIGIN Medial epicondyle of humerus

INSERTION Distal collateral tubercles of proximal phalanx; proximal collateral tubercles of middle phalanx

INNERVATION Ulnar nerve

FUNCTION Flexes digit and carpus; extends elbow

DEVELOPMENT ISSUES Injury generally to tendon of insertion; muscle usually spasms when tendon injured

DEEP DIGITAL FLEXOR

a. humeral head (Figure 2.13)

ORIGIN Medial epicondyle of humerus

INSERTION Flexor surface of distal phalanx

INNERVATION Median and ulnar nerves

FUNCTION Flexes digit and carpus; extends elbow

DEVELOPMENT ISSUES Pathology usually occurs between tendon of insertion and navicular bursa

b. ulnar head (Figure 2.13)

ORIGIN Medial on olecranon

INSERTION Flexor surface of distal phalanx

INNERVATION Ulnar nerve

FUNCTION Flexes digit and carpus; extends elbow

c. radial head (not shown)

ORIGIN Mid-caudal surface of radius

INSERTION Flexor surface of distal phalanx

INNERVATION Median nerve

FUNCTION Flexes digit and carpus; extends elbow

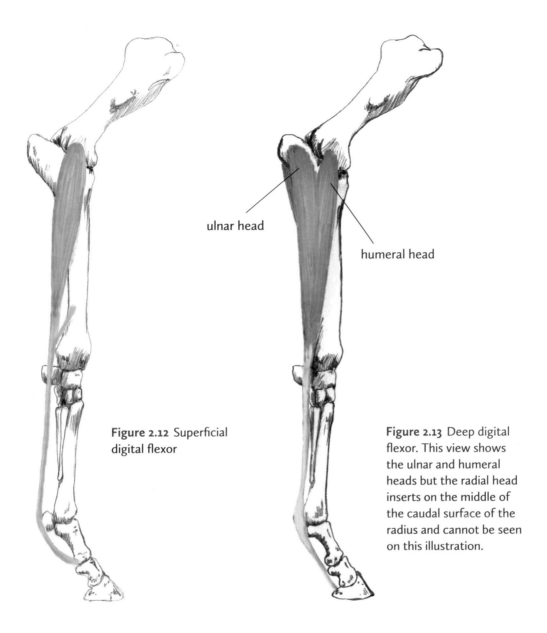

ulnar head

humeral head

Figure 2.12 Superficial digital flexor

Figure 2.13 Deep digital flexor. This view shows the ulnar and humeral heads but the radial head inserts on the middle of the caudal surface of the radius and cannot be seen on this illustration.

FLEXOR CARPI ULNARIS

a. humeral head (Figure 2.14)

ORIGIN Medial epicondyle of humerus

INSERTION Accessory carpal bone

INNERVATION Ulnar nerve

FUNCTION Flexes carpus

DEVELOPMENT ISSUES Horse drags toe on affected side

b. ulnar head (Figure 2.14)

ORIGIN Medial olecranon

INSERTION Accessory carpal bone

INNERVATION Ulnar nerve

FUNCTION Flexes carpus

DEVELOPMENT ISSUES Horse drags toe on affected side

FLEXOR CARPI RADIALIS (Figure 2.15)

ORIGIN Medial epicondyle of humerus

INSERTION Proximal metacarpal 2

INNERVATION Median nerve

FUNCTION Flexes carpus

DEVELOPMENT ISSUES As above

METACARPUS

INTEROSSEUS (SUSPENSORY LIGAMENT) (Figure 2.16)

ORIGIN Proximocaudal on 3rd metacarpal bone (MC3) and palmar carpal ligament

INSERTION Proximal sesamoid bones. Tendons bifurcate from insertion to insert on common digital extensor tendon

INNERVATION Deep ulnar nerve

FUNCTION Prevents overextension of fetlock

DEVELOPMENT ISSUES Lameness

Below the knee there is no muscle (the interosseus has evolved to be a passive elastic spring). However, there are important ligaments associated with the fetlock, namely the straight and cruciate ligaments (Figure 2.17 – the cruciate ligaments are in orange and the straight ligaments are in brown).

These sesamoidean ligaments are clinically important in athletic horses. They are a common site of injury (desmitis) and result in a low to moderate degree of lameness.

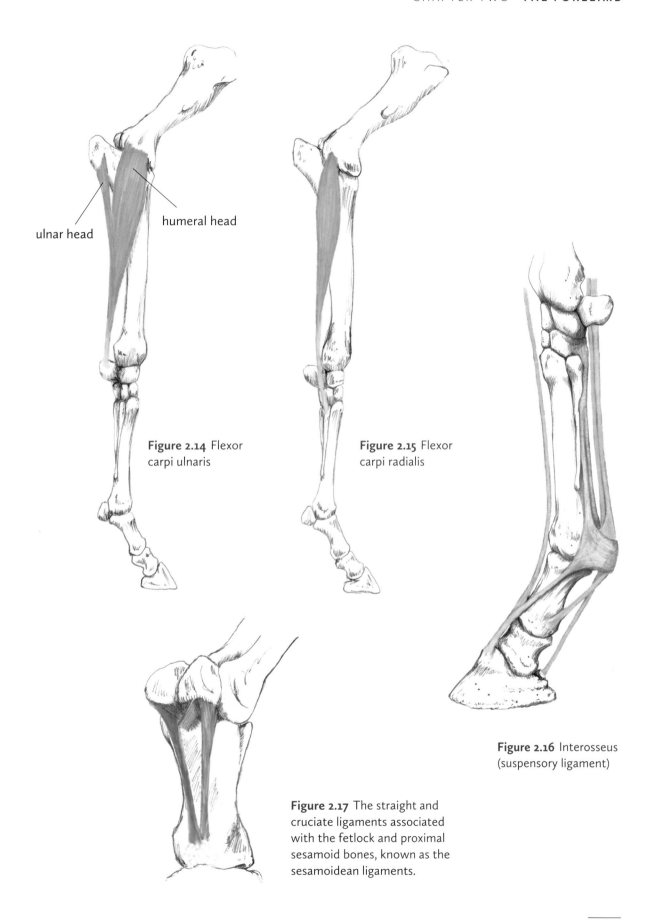

ulnar head

humeral head

Figure 2.14 Flexor carpi ulnaris

Figure 2.15 Flexor carpi radialis

Figure 2.16 Interosseus (suspensory ligament)

Figure 2.17 The straight and cruciate ligaments associated with the fetlock and proximal sesamoid bones, known as the sesamoidean ligaments.

CRANIOLATERAL FOREARM

COMMON DIGITAL EXTENSOR

a. radial head (not shown)

ORIGIN Lateral epicondyle of humerus

INSERTION Proximodorsal on proximal phalanx

INNERVATION Radial nerve

FUNCTION Carpal and digital extensor

DEVELOPMENT ISSUES Stumbling or dragging of toe

b. humeral head (Figure 2.18)

ORIGIN Lateral epicondyle of humerus

INSERTION Extensor process of distal phalanx

INNERVATION Radial nerve

FUNCTION Carpal and digital extensor

DEVELOPMENT ISSUES As above

c. ulnar head (not shown)

ORIGIN Lateral epicondyle of humerus

INSERTION Extensor process of distal phalanx

INNERVATION Radial nerve

FUNCTION Carpal and digital extensor

DEVELOPMENT ISSUES As above

LATERAL DIGITAL EXTENSOR (Figure 2.19)

ORIGIN Proximal radius and ulna

INSERTION Proximodorsal on proximal phalanx

INNERVATION Radial nerve

FUNCTION Extends fetlock

DEVELOPMENT ISSUES As above

EXTENSOR CARPI RADIALIS (Figure 2.20)

ORIGIN Lateral supracondylar crest and radial fossa

INSERTION Proximodorsal on 3rd metacarpal bone (MC3)

INNERVATION Radial nerve

FUNCTION Extends carpus

DEVELOPMENT ISSUES Unlevelness

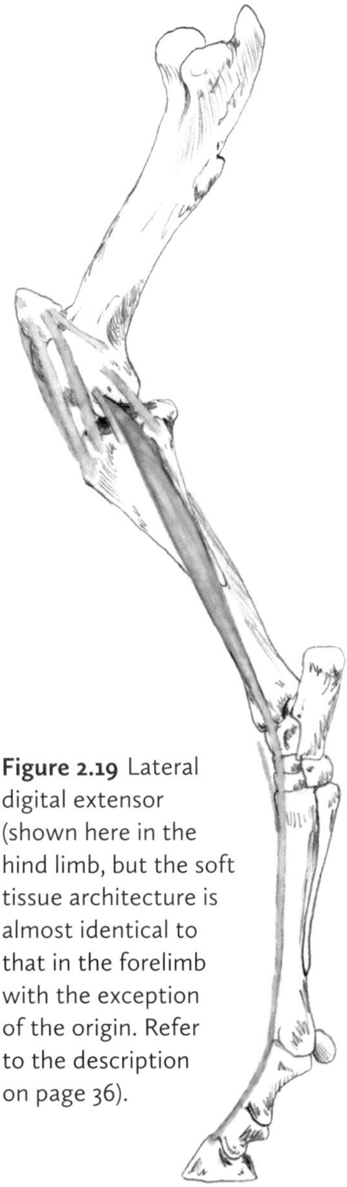

Figure 2.19 Lateral digital extensor (shown here in the hind limb, but the soft tissue architecture is almost identical to that in the forelimb with the exception of the origin. Refer to the description on page 36).

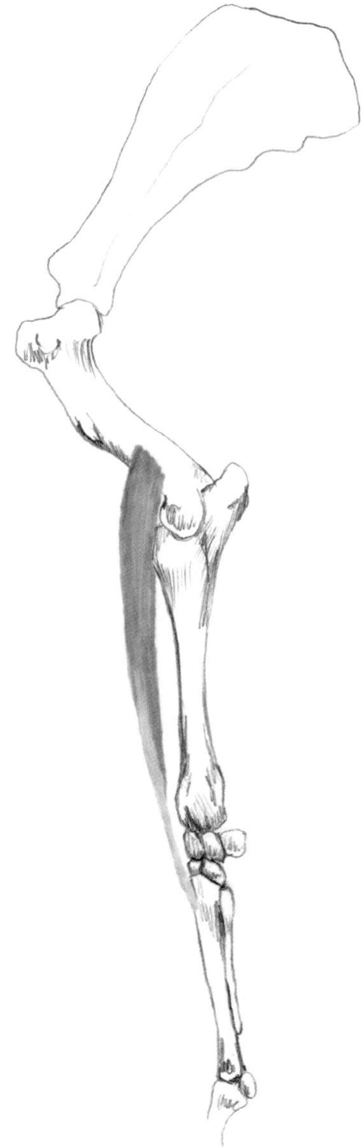

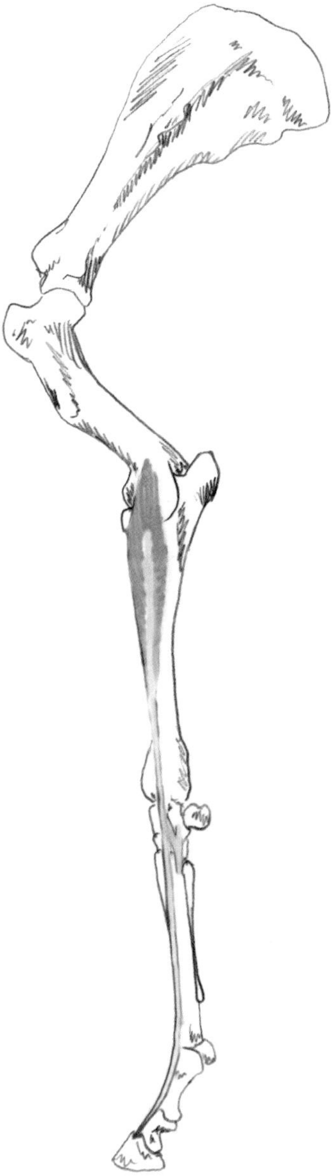

Figure 2.18 Common digital extensor. Only the humeral head of this muscle is illustrated because the radial and ulnar heads are deep to this muscle and are not shown in this illustration.

Figure 2.20 Extensor carpi radialis

ULNARIS LATERALIS (Figure 2.21)

ORIGIN Lateral epicondyle of humerus

INSERTION Short tendon on accessory carpal bone; long tendon proximally on 4th metacarpal

INNERVATION Radial nerve

FUNCTION Flexes carpus

Stay apparatus

The horse is perfectly capable of dozing whilst standing up, but to truly rest he lies down. Why should he have evolved to sleep standing up? Again, the answer is that he is a prey animal, and if he is already standing up when he senses a predator, he can just gallop away without wasting time getting to his feet. If you have observed a horse rising from a recumbent position, you will know that it is not a particularly speedy process, and should he have been lying down when the predator approaches, he may well have become someone's supper before he even gets on his feet. Therefore, horses only tend to lie down at night when they are unobserved.

The four legs of the horse are angulated bony columns, which normally if not under conscious control, would collapse. In Chapter 1 we explained about elastic energy and how tendinous structures within certain muscles of the horse are there as simple passive springs to aid locomotion. However, they also have another function within what is known as the 'stay apparatus' (Figure 2.22). The stay apparatus is the anatomical means by which the horse can rest in a standing position without the joints collapsing due to relaxed muscle tone. Many of the structures within the stay apparatus contain tendinous tissue and because they act as tendinous springs, once they have reached their maximum length, they become stable. Also, because they are non-fatiguing tissue no real energetic input is required.

The first major muscle involved in the stay apparatus is the serratus ventralis muscle (see Chapter 4 Figure 4.23) which is the principle muscle of weight bearing of the thorax. It is heavily interlaced with tendinous tissue so that, once limbs are stabilised, the horse can simply settle the weight of the thorax into the serratus ventralis.

Stablising front limbs starts with the shoulder joint, which is largely restricted to flexion and extension because of the stabilising effect of the supraspinatus and infraspinatus laterally, and the subscapularis medially.

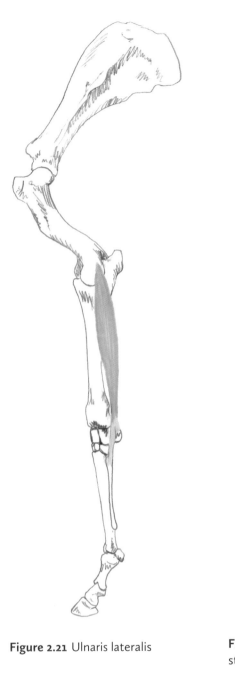

Figure 2.21 Ulnaris lateralis

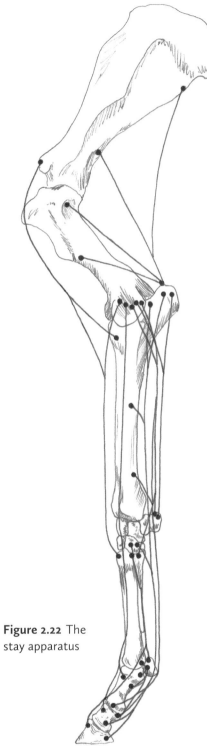

Figure 2.22 The stay apparatus

The primary stabiliser of the shoulder is the biceps brachii, the tendon of origin of which presses against the front of the shoulder joint. As the horse relaxes his body, the shoulder joint flexes, but as it does so the tendon of the biceps tightens. As this happens, the first insertion of the biceps (just below the front of the elbow joint) pulls the elbow cranially, i.e. it pulls it forwards to stabilise the joint, and prevents it from flexing.

Another tendinous portion of the biceps brachii fuses with lacertus fibrosus and extensor carpi radialis, which then stabilises the knee.

The elbow is principally stabilised by the carpal and digital flexors which also contain much fibrous tissue. Whether the triceps also play a part in the stay apparatus is still widely contentious. Many believe that because of the lack of increased tonus in this muscle whilst the rest of the stay apparatus is in use, then it cannot be playing any part in shoulder stabilisation.

The knee is prevented from flexing by the biceps brachii (see page 27) acting on the extensor surface of the knee, but also by the flexor carpi ulnaris and ulnaris lateralis (which attach to the accessory carpal bone) that come under tension by the weight of the trunk via the fixed shoulder joint. This exerts a caudal pull on the flexor surface of the knee to prevent knee flexion. This is aided by the accessory (check) ligaments of the deep and superficial digital flexors.

Suspensory apparatus

The suspensory apparatus is all tendinous/ligamentous tissue with no muscle fibres to fatigue. The suspensory apparatus is also present in the hind limb (see Chapter 3). The fetlock needs to be supported to prevent overextension when the horse relaxes and brings the stay apparatus into action. Therefore the fetlock needs to be 'suspended' and this is where the suspensory ligament comes into play. Technically the suspensory ligament is a muscle (interosseus – see Figure 2.16) but it has evolved into a passive tendinous spring. The branches of the suspensory ligament are really the tendons of insertion of the interosseus muscle. As the horse's weight settles into the fetlock, it is prevented from overextending not only by the suspensory ligament, but also by the tendons of the superficial and deep digital flexor muscles.

The equine forelimb is therefore a highly complicated functional structure designed to support the majority of the horse's weight, whilst at the same time providing optimum, energy-saving performance.

CHAPTER THREE

The Hind Limb

Whist the forelimb is mainly concerned with support, the hind limb is for propulsion. It is the structure that drives the horse forwards. Straightened out, the hind limb of the horse is functionally longer than the forelimb because it is the 'powerhouse' that drives the horse forwards. Also the hind hooves are a different shape to those of the front limbs. Whilst the front hooves are wider and rounder to help support the weight of the forehand, the hind hooves are longer and more pointed to enable the toes to penetrate the ground giving the horse a firm base against which to propel the body forwards. In this chapter we will illustrate and describe the major muscles of the hind limb and the structures that enable the horse to sleep standing up and rest a hind limb whilst so doing. These are the **reciprocal apparatus** and the **stifle locking mechanism**.

Muscles of the hind limb

MUSCLES OF THE HIP JOINT

TENSOR FASCIAE LATAE Figure 3.1

ORIGIN Tuber coxa

INSERTION a. Third trochanter (with superficial gluteal muscle); b. with fascia lata on patella, lateral patellar ligament and cranial border of tibia

INNERVATION Cranial gluteal nerve

FUNCTION a. Flexes hip; b. extends stifle; c. protracts hind limb; d. tenses fascia lata

DEVELOPMENT ISSUES Relatively few, most trauma based

SUPERFICIAL GLUTEAL (Figure 3.2)

ORIGIN Tuber coxa

INSERTION Third trochanter and fascia lata

INNERVATION Cranial and caudal gluteal nerve

FUNCTION a. Flexes hip; b. abducts (moves away from body) and protracts hind limb

DEVELOPMENT ISSUES Reduced step length; resists lateral movement

MIDDLE GLUTEAL (Figure 3.3)

ORIGIN a. Longissimus lumborum; b. gluteal surface of ilium; c. sacrum; d. sacroiliac and sacrosciatic ligaments

INSERTION Greater trochanter at head of femur

INNERVATION Cranial gluteal nerve

FUNCTION a. Extends hip; b. abducts hind limb

DEVELOPMENT ISSUES As above

ACCESSORY GLUTEAL (Figure 3.4)

ORIGIN Gluteal surface of ilium

INSERTION Distal to greater trochanter

INNERVATION Cranial gluteal nerve

FUNCTION a. Extends hip; b. abducts hind limb

DEVELOPMENT ISSUES As above

DEEP GLUTEAL (Figure 3.5)

ORIGIN Spine of ischia

INSERTION Greater trochanter at head of femur

INNERVATION Cranial gluteal nerve

FUNCTION Abducts hind limb

DEVELOPMENT ISSUES As above

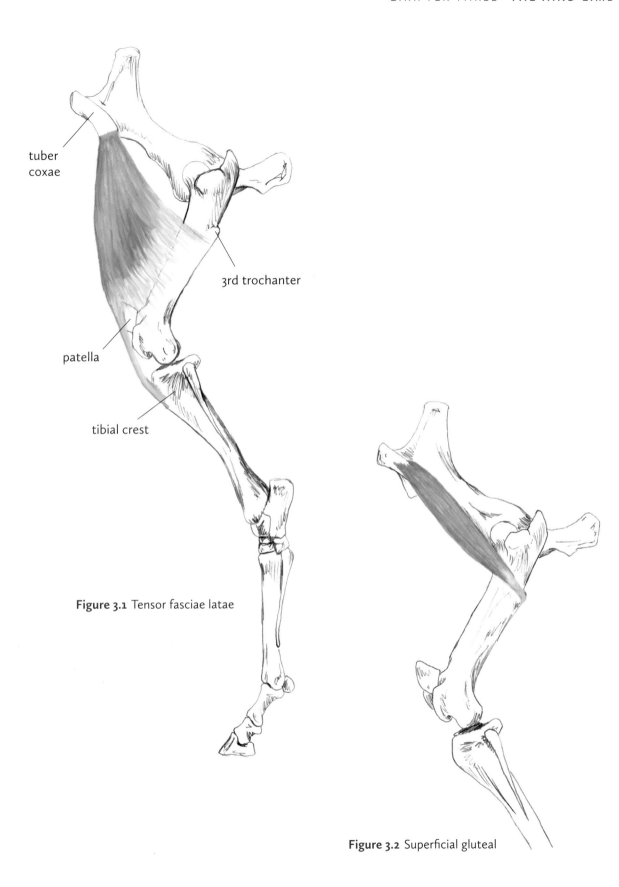

tuber
coxae

3rd trochanter

patella

tibial crest

Figure 3.1 Tensor fasciae latae

Figure 3.2 Superficial gluteal

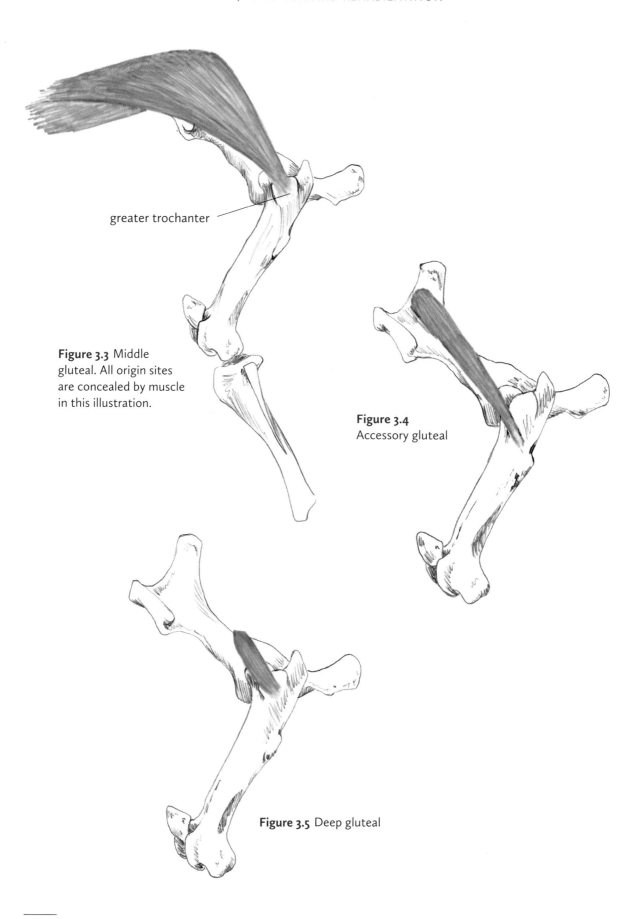

greater trochanter

Figure 3.3 Middle gluteal. All origin sites are concealed by muscle in this illustration.

Figure 3.4 Accessory gluteal

Figure 3.5 Deep gluteal

CAUDAL THIGH MUSCLES (HAMSTRINGS GROUP)

BICEPS FEMORIS (Figure 3.6)

ORIGIN a. Vertebral head: spinous and transverse processes of last three sacral vertebrae, sacrosciatic ligament and tail fascia; b. pelvic head: tuber ischia

INSERTION a. Patella, lateral and middle patella ligaments; b. cranial border of tibia and crural fascia; c. via long calcanean tendon to calcaneus

INNERVATION Caudal gluteal and sciatic nerves

FUNCTION a. Extends hip and stifle; b. with caudal division flexes stifle; c. abducts hind limb

DEVELOPMENT ISSUES Shortening of cranial portion of stride; resists lateral movement; discomfort in hind joints

SEMITENDINOSUS (Figure 3.7)

ORIGIN a. Vertebral head: last sacral and first two caudal vertebrae, tail fascia and sacrosciatic ligament; b. pelvic head: ventral tuber ischia

INSERTION a. Cranial border of tibia, crural fascia; b. via long calcanean tendon to calcanius

INNERVATION Caudal gluteal and sciatic nerves

FUNCTION a. During weight bearing: extends hip, stifle and hock; b. During non-weight bearing: retracts and adducts limb

DEVELOPMENT ISSUES As above

SEMIMEMBRANOSUS (Figure 3.8)

ORIGIN a. Vertebral head: first caudal vertebra, sacrosciatic ligament; b. pelvic head: ventromedial aspect of tuber ischia

INSERTION Medial condyles of femur and tibia

INNERVATION Caudal gluteal and sciatic nerves

FUNCTION a. During weight bearing: extends hip and stifle; b. during non-weight bearing: retracts and adducts limb

DEVELOPMENT ISSUES As above

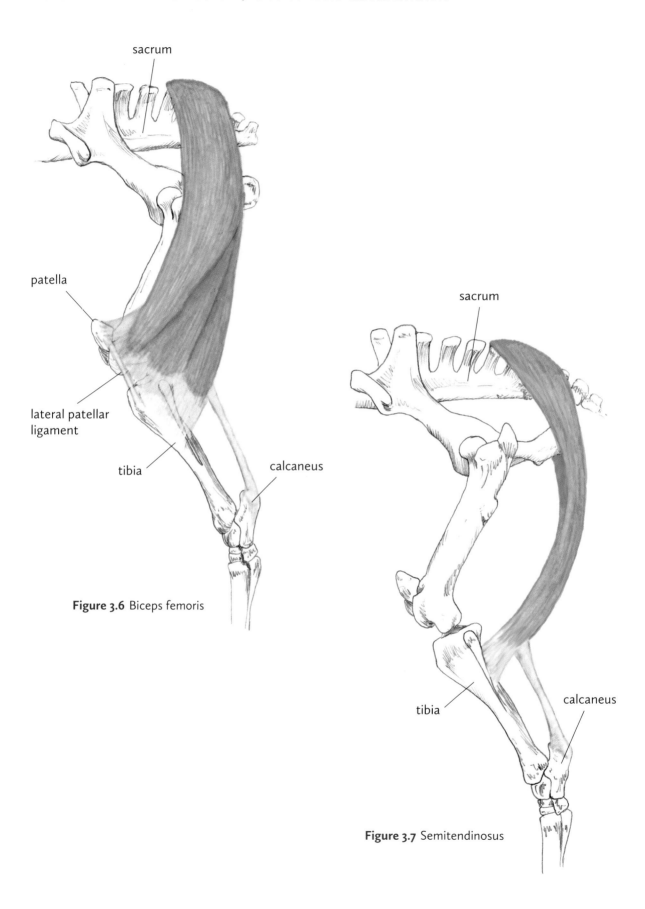

sacrum

patella

lateral patellar
ligament

tibia

calcaneus

Figure 3.6 Biceps femoris

sacrum

tibia

calcaneus

Figure 3.7 Semitendinosus

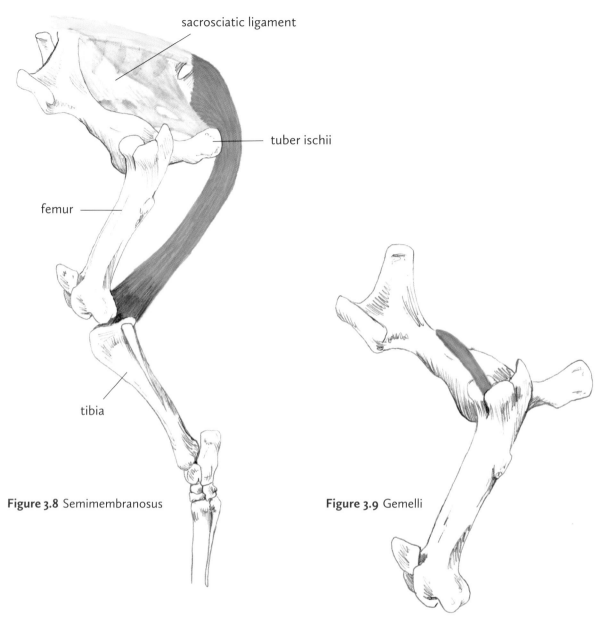

sacrosciatic ligament

tuber ischii

femur

tibia

Figure 3.8 Semimembranosus

Figure 3.9 Gemelli

DEEP MUSCLES OF THE HIP

GEMELLI (Figure 3.9)

ORIGIN Dorsal border of ischium

INSERTION Trocanteric fossa of femur

INNERVATION Sciatic nerve

FUNCTION Rotates femur laterally

DEVELOPMENT ISSUES Overreaching injuries on front limb; moving on three tracks

INTERNAL OBTURATOR (Figure 3.10)

ORIGIN Internal surface of ischium and pubis from border of obturator foramen to pelvic symphysis

INSERTION Trocanteric fossa of femur

INNERVATION Sciatic nerve

FUNCTION Rotates femur laterally

DEVELOPMENT ISSUES Overreaching injuries on front limb; moving on three tracks

EXTERNAL OBTURATOR (Figure 3.11)

ORIGIN Ventral surface of pelvis from border of obturator foramen

INSERTION Trocanteric fossa of femur

INNERVATION Obturator nerve

FUNCTION Rotates femur laterally and adducts limb

DEVELOPMENT ISSUES As above plus horse resists lateral work

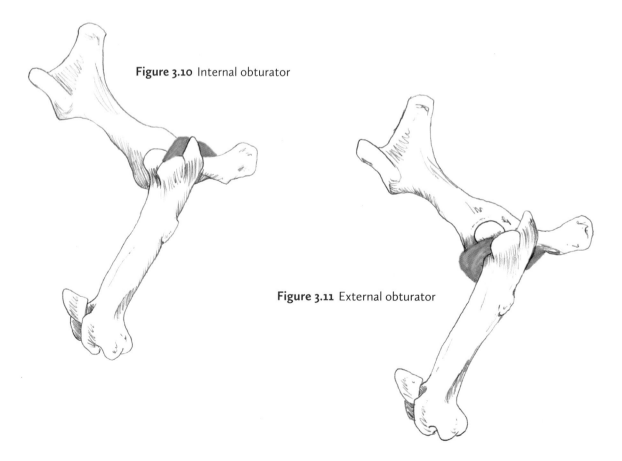

Figure 3.10 Internal obturator

Figure 3.11 External obturator

MEDIAL MUSCLES OF THE THIGH

GRACILIS (Figure 3.12)

ORIGIN Pelvic symphysis via symphysial tendon

INSERTION Crural fascia, medial patella ligament, cranial border of tibia

INNERVATION Obturator nerve

FUNCTION Adducts limb

DEVELOPMENT Resists lateral work

ADDUCTOR (Figure 3.13)

ORIGIN Ventral surface of pelvis; symphysial tendon

INSERTION Caudal surface and medial epicondyle of femur

INNERVATION Obturator nerve

FUNCTION Adducts and retracts limb

DEVELOPMENT ISSUES As above

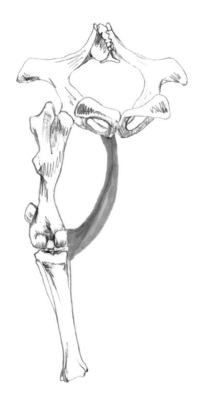 

Figure 3.12 Gracilis

Figure 3.13 Adductor

Figure 3.14 Pectineus

PECTINEUS (Figure 3.14)

ORIGIN Pubis and iliopubic eminence

INSERTION Medial surface of femur

INNERVATION Obturator nerve and femoral nerve

FUNCTION Adducts limb; flexes hip joint

DEVELOPMENT ISSUES Resists lateral work

STIFLE EXTENSORS

SARTORIUS (Figure 3.15)

ORIGIN Iliac fascia and insertion tendon of psoas minor

INSERTION Medial aspect of stifle

INNERVATION Femoral nerve

FUNCTION Flexes hip; protracts and adducts limb

DEVELOPMENT ISSUES Unlevelness; resistance to lateral work

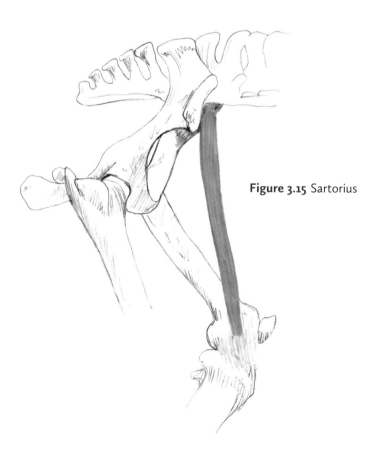

Figure 3.15 Sartorius

QUADRICEPS FEMORIS (Figures 3.16a and b)

a. rectus femoris (Figure 3.16a)

ORIGIN Shaft of ilium cranial to acetabulum

b. vastus lateralis (Figure 3.16a)

ORIGIN Proximolateral on femur

c. vastus medialis (Figure 3.16b)

ORIGIN Proximomedial on femur

d. vastus intermedius (not shown)

ORIGIN Proximodorsal on femur

INSERTION Via intermediate patellar ligament on tibial tuberosity

INNERVATION Femoral nerve

FUNCTION Flexes hip, extends and stabilises stifle

DEVELOPMENT ISSUES Unlevelness; resistance to lateral work

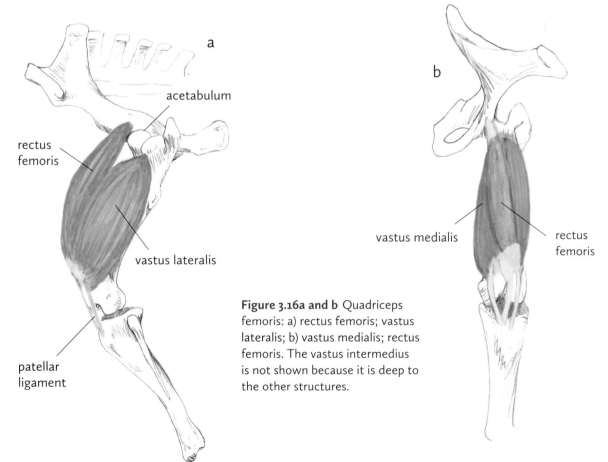

Figure 3.16a and b Quadriceps femoris: a) rectus femoris; vastus lateralis; b) vastus medialis; rectus femoris. The vastus intermedius is not shown because it is deep to the other structures.

STIFLE FLEXOR

POPLITEUS (Figure 3.17)

ORIGIN Lateral condyle of femur

INSERTION Caudomedial border of tibia

INNERVATION Tibial nerve

FUNCTION Flexes stifle

DEVELOPMENT ISSUES Unlevelness; dragging of toe

HOCK EXTENSORS AND DIGIT FLEXORS (CAUDAL)

GASTROCNEMIUS (Figure 3.18)

ORIGIN Supracondylar tuberosities of the femur

INSERTION Via long calcanean tendon onto calcaneus

INNERVATION Tibial nerve

FUNCTION Extends hock and flexes stifle

DEVELOPMENT ISSUES Unlevelness; shortness of step; dragging of toe

SUPERFICIAL DIGITAL FLEXOR
(Figure 3.19 – see also reciprocal apparatus on page 58 and Figure 3.26)

ORIGIN Supracondylar fossa of femur

INSERTION Plantar on distal end of proximal phalanx and proximal collateral tubercles of middle phalanx

INNERVATION Tibial nerve

FUNCTION Proximally acts as part of reciprocal apparatus

DEVELOPMENT ISSUES Little if any muscle tissue: evolved as passive spring; injury mainly as a result of trauma

DEEP DIGITAL FLEXOR (Figure 3.20)

a. lateral digital flexor

ORIGIN Caudal surface of tibia with tibialis caudalis

b. tibialis caudalis

ORIGIN Caudal surface of tibia with lateral digital flexor

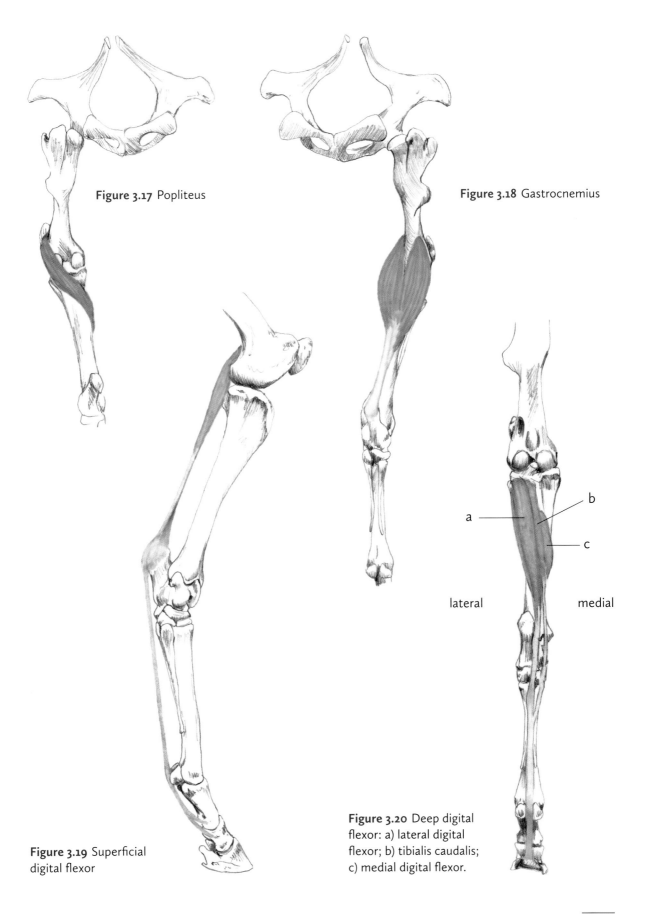

Figure 3.17 Popliteus

Figure 3.18 Gastrocnemius

a

b

c

lateral   medial

Figure 3.19 Superficial
digital flexor

Figure 3.20 Deep digital
flexor: a) lateral digital
flexor; b) tibialis caudalis;
c) medial digital flexor.

c. medial digital flexor

ORIGIN Lateral tibial condyle

INSERTION Plantar on distal phalanx

INNERVATION Tibial nerve

FUNCTION Extends hock and flexes digit

DEVELOPMENT ISSUES Unlevelness; dragging of toe

HOCK FLEXORS AND DIGIT EXTENSORS

TIBIALIS CRANIALIS (Figure 3.21)

ORIGIN Lateral condyle and tuberosity of tibia

INSERTION a. Dorsal branch on proximal end of 3rd metatarsal and 3rd tarsal bone b. medial branch on 1st and 2nd tarsal bone

INNERVATION Peroneal nerve

FUNCTION Flexes hock

DEVELOPMENT ISSUES Short stride cranially

PERONEUS TERTIUS (Figure 3.22)

ORIGIN Lateral condyle of femur

INSERTION Tarsal bones (except 1 and 2) and on 3rd metatarsal

INNERVATION Peroneal nerve

FUNCTION Entirely tendinous and forms reciprocal apparatus with superficial digital flexor

DEVELOPMENT ISSUES Usually traumatic only

LATERAL DIGITAL EXTENSOR (Figure 3.23)

ORIGIN Lateral collateral ligament of stifle and adjacent tibia and fibula

INSERTION Joins tendon of long extensor

INNERVATION Peroneal nerve

FUNCTION Extends digit and flexes hock

DEVELOPMENT ISSUES Short stride cranially and dragging of toe

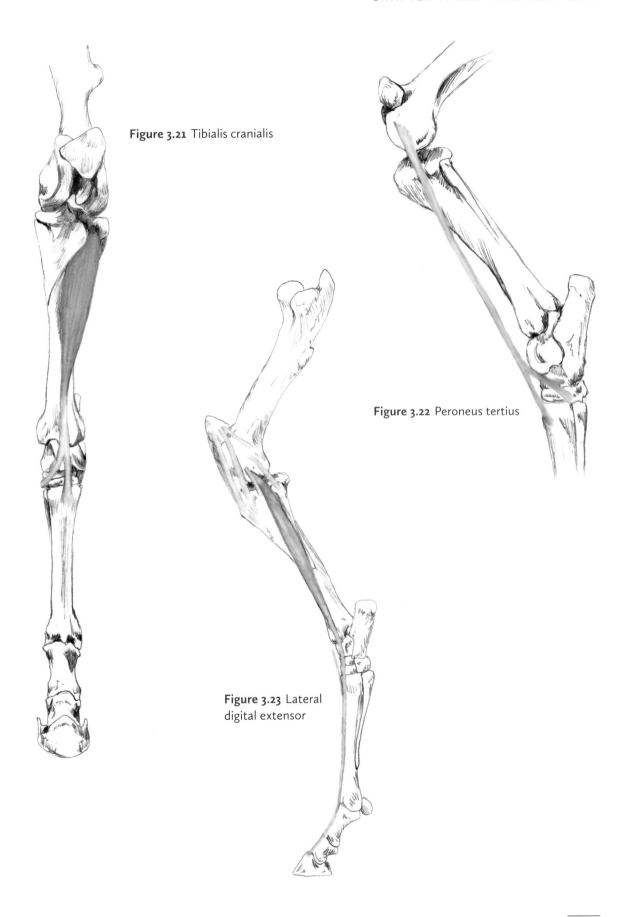

Figure 3.21 Tibialis cranialis

Figure 3.22 Peroneus tertius

Figure 3.23 Lateral
digital extensor

METATARSUS

INTERROSEUS (SUSPENSORY LIGAMENT) (Figure 3.24)

ORIGIN 3rd metacarpal, calcaneus and 4th tarsal bone

INSERTION Proximal sesamoid bones

INNERVATION Tibial nerve

FUNCTION Counteracts overextension of fetlock

DEVELOPMENT ISSUES Usually at origin in horses worked on deep rubber surfaces

In the hind limb, the structures below the fetlock have the same configuration as the forelimb including the sesamoidean ligaments (see Chapter 2).

Like the forelimb, the hind limb also contains suspensory apparatus using the same structures as in the forelimb. However, the hind limb also contains two other specialised energy-saving systems which fix the hind limb to enable the horse to sleep standing up: the **stifle locking mechanism** and **reciprocal apparatus**.

Stifle locking mechanism

The stifle locking mechanism (Figure 3.25) enables the horse to lock the stifle out completely, preventing any flexion during muscle relaxation on rest. The group of muscles that perform this action comprise the quadriceps femoris and tensor fasciae latae, which have insertions on the intermediate patellar ligament. When contracted, with the limb weight bearing, they pull the patella, the parapatellar cartilage and the medial patellar ligament inwards and upwards and 'hook' them over the medial trochlear ridge of the femur. This prevents the stifle joint from flexing. The horse will rest the other hind limb by slightly flexing the joints and resting on the toe. To return the stifle to normal movement, the horse contracts the quadriceps and lifts the patella off the trochlear ridge. You can observe this in the resting, standing horse when he is resting one hind limb, and locking the stifle of the other hind limb. However, some muscular effort must be required for this process as the horse will tire of standing on one hind limb after a few minutes and will change to lock the opposite hind limb whilst resting the one that had previously been locked.

Figure 3.24 Interroseus
(suspensory ligament)

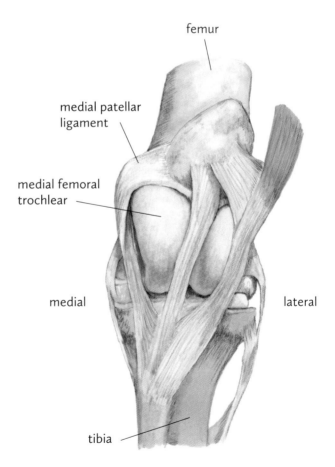

femur

medial patellar
ligament

medial femoral
trochlear

medial

lateral

tibia

Figure 3.25 The stifle locking
mechanism, left hind dorsal view.

Sometimes (particularly in fast-growing warmblood breeds) this can happen during movement. This leads to the condition known as 'locking stifle', which is also known as upward patellar fixation, in which the hind limb locks out during normal movement, without conscious effort by the horse. Usually, by making the horse walk backwards, the stifle will unlock, but it can be a distressing condition for horse and owner. Normally, as the horse gets stronger, the syndrome will resolve completely without any intervention, but in some cases surgery may be indicated. Locking stifle is a condition that very often responds to skilled physiotherapy treatment.

Reciprocal apparatus

In the absence of trauma, the horse cannot flex or extend the stifle without flexing or extending the hock – the two are inextricably linked by a system known as the reciprocal apparatus (Figure 3.26). This comprises two muscles, the superficial digital flexor muscle (see page 52), and the peroneus tertius muscle (see page 54). Because of the action of these two muscles the

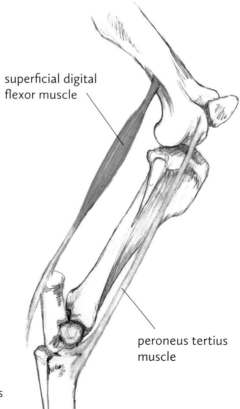

superficial digital flexor muscle

peroneus tertius muscle

Figure 3.26 The reciprocal apparatus

movement of the two joints mirror each other. However, neither of these structures are strictly muscles. The peroneus tertius is entirely tendinous and the superficial digital flexor has very little muscle tissue within it; it has evolved to become a passive spring. Therefore the stifle and the hock must move in unison. It follows that if the stifle is locked by the locking mechanism then, because of the reciprocal apparatus, the hock is also locked.

Chapters 2 and 3 should have ensured you now have an appreciation of how the limbs of the appendicular skeleton work, and just how fragile they can be, especially below the knee and hock.

CHAPTER FOUR

The Axial Skeleton

T HE FUNCTIONAL ANATOMY of the neck and back of the horse (the axial skeleton) is something that is now attracting a good deal of interest and research. Gone (hopefully) are the days when we simply labeled the horse as 'cold backed' if he dipped or put his back up when putting on a saddle or mounting. We now understand that cold backed simply means pain, which needs to be addressed by your veterinary surgeon and your physiotherapist.

We also know that what we used to term 'bridle lame' is also a pain response to being ridden, and that pathology in the neck and back can cause lameness that may manifest in another area of the body, and often cause behavioural changes. When you have neck or back pain, the last thing you want to do is exercise and flex those areas of your body. And yet some riders and ill-informed instructors will still put these manifestations of pain down to resistance or bad temperament, and will attempt to over-use spurs and/or whips on the horse to 'adjust his attitude'. Remember that pain is one of the three most common reasons for your horse not doing what you want him to do, so causing him more pain with whips and spurs is unlikely to help the situation. And horses that are normally biddable do not suddenly develop a bad attitude.

If pain is manifesting itself as limb lameness, then it is very often the case that the rider or trainer can see the necessity for treatment that may include rest. So it still remains a mystery why they will very often not accept that their horse is displaying signs of pain in the neck and back which similarly need treatment and rest. In the experience of most vets and physiotherapists this is simply because of a lack of knowledge by the owner or trainer, rather than unkindness. Also, in Chapter 1 it was explained that, as a prey animal, horses will disguise pain until it becomes impossible to continue, and some very stoic horses can disguise pain in the neck and back for a long time before it becomes manifest.

In this chapter we explain the way the back is put together and how it should work because, if it goes wrong, then the whole horse becomes wrong and without understanding the system you could be causing immeasurable discomfort and athletic impairment.

Structure

The equine vertebral column follows the same general structure as all veterinary mammals. There are cervical (neck) vertebrae, thoracic (those to which ribs are connected) vertebrae, lumbar (lower back) vertebrae, sacral (base of spine) vertebrae and caudal (tail) vertebrae (Figure 4.1). Abbreviations for these vertebrae are: cervical – C; thoracic – T; lumbar – L; sacral – S; caudal – CD.

In the horse there are 7 cervical, 18 thoracic, 6 lumbar and 5 sacral vertebrae, and they have functional mechanics that are specific to the horse

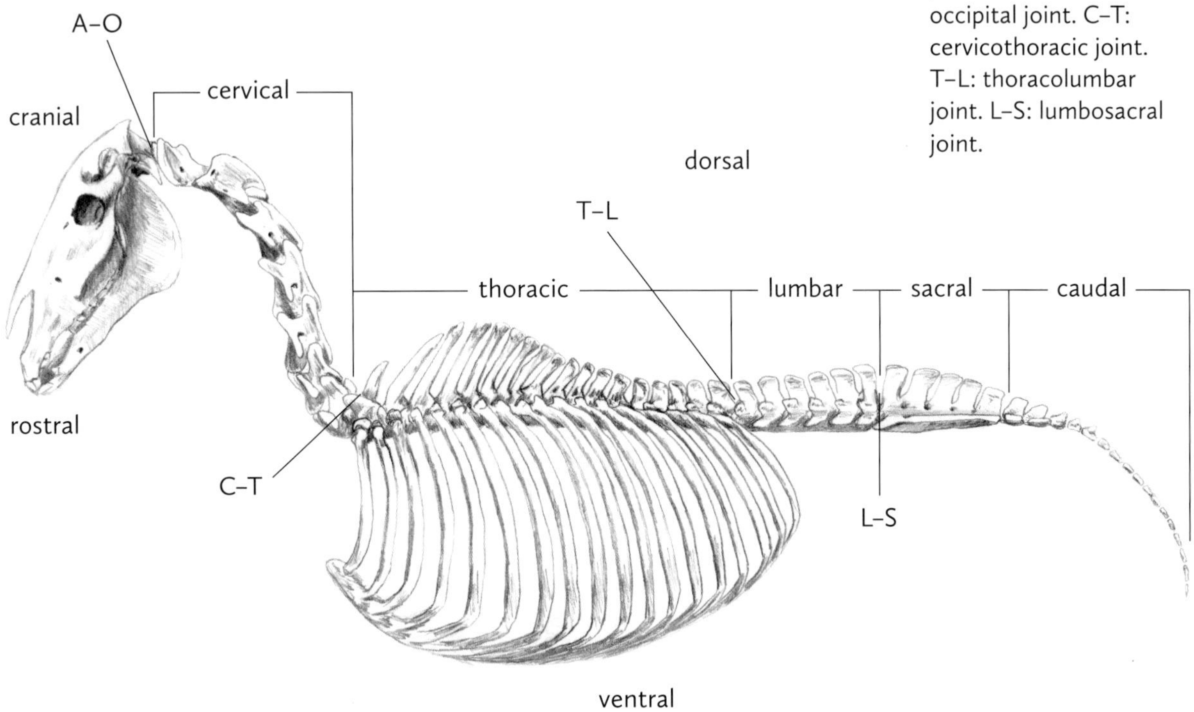

Figure 4.1 The equine vertebral column (axial skeleton) showing the vertebral categories and the inter-vertebral joints. A–O: atlanto-occipital joint. C–T: cervicothoracic joint. T–L: thoracolumbar joint. L–S: lumbosacral joint.

as a prey animal. It is this structure of the axial skeleton that allows us to ride the horse. If his back moved in the same way as a cat or dog (a predator), then we would not be able to use him for weight carrying. You only have to look at the differences between the flexibility of the spine between a dog and a horse when they are in full flight (Photo 4.2).

There is surprisingly little movement in the joints between the vertebrae in the horse. Much of the movement in any direction comes from the neck, and the central portion of the thorax. It may come as a complete surprise to readers that there is little movement at all behind the saddle in the horse. Because the horse is a prey animal there are very good evolutionary reasons for this in biomechanical terms.

Figures 4.3 to 4.5 (see pages 63, 64 and 65) show the intervertebral joint movement in the equine back. These intervertebral joint movements have been measured in all three planes – flexion and extension (rounding and hollowing); axial rotation (twisting) and lateral flexion (sideways bending).

For the purposes of this book, the vertebral column has been divided into distinct functional sections, so that a complete understanding of the functional anatomy of the back can be given.

Photo 4.2 The difference between equine and canine back movements.

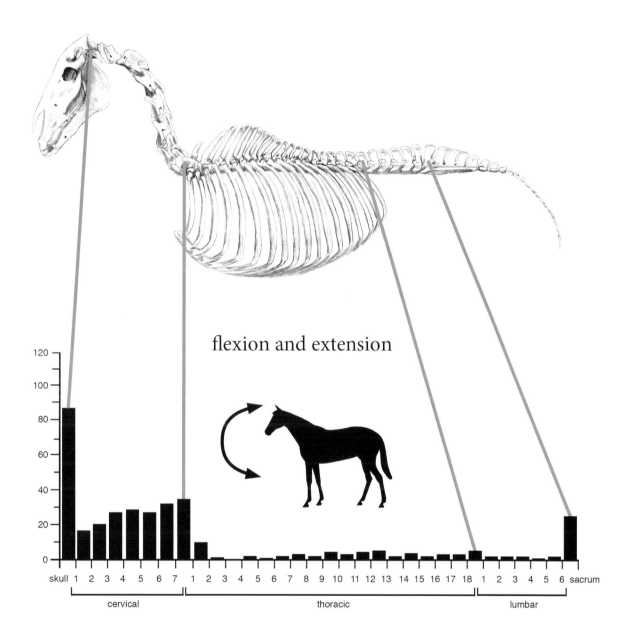

flexion and extension

Figure 4.3 Movement in flexion and extension (rounding and hollowing). Each of the bars on the graph relate to the amount of movement in the corresponding intervertebral joint. Note there is little movement in any of the joints except in the neck and in the lumbosacral joint. (Graph section courtesy of Professor Hilary Clayton)

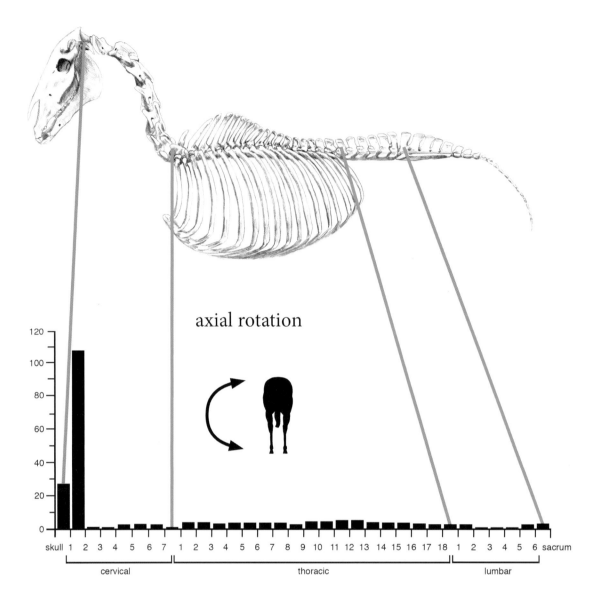

axial rotation

Figure 4.4 *above* Movement in axial rotation (twisting around the spine). Each of the bars on the graph relate to the amount of movement in the corresponding intervertebral joint. (Graph section courtesy of Professor Hilary Clayton)

Figure 4.5 *opposite page* Movement in lateral flexion (bending to the left and right). Each of the bars on the graph relate to the amount of movement in the corresponding intervertebral joint. (Graph section courtesy of Professor Hilary Clayton)

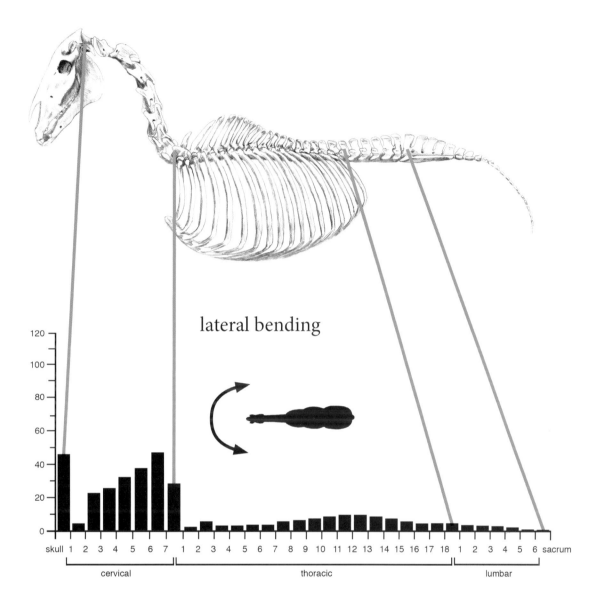

lateral bending

Neck

Atlanto-occipital joint

As can be seen, the neck has a lot of movements in all planes except for twisting, but the first two intervertebral joints , the atlanto-occipital joint (C1/2) and the atlanto-axial joint (C2/3) have very specific movement planes. In flexion and extension there is a considerable amount of movement in the former and not much in the latter. As this equates to nodding it is sometimes referred to as the 'yes' joint. The muscles responsible for this movement are the **splenius** and **rectus capitus dorsalis**, which lift the head up, and the **longus capitus** and the **rectus capitus ventralis** which flex the head down.

SPLENIUS (Figure 4.6)

ORIGIN Spinous processes of T3–5 by means of thoracolumbar fascia; nuchal ligament

INSERTION Nuchal crest and mastoid process of temporal bone; transverse spinous processes C2–5

INNERVATION Dorsal branch of local spinal nerve and dorsal branch of accessory nerve

FUNCTION Extends, lifts or bends neck and head laterally

DEVELOPMENT ISSUES Neck stiff in lateral flexion

RECTUS CAPITUS DORSALIS (Figure 4.7)

ORIGIN Spinous process of axis

INSERTION Nuchal crest

INNERVATION Dorsal branch of C1

FUNCTION Elevates head

DEVELOPMENT ISSUES Horse does not take contact; fights hand

LONGUS CAPITUS (Figure 4.8)

ORIGIN Transverse processes C3–5

INSERTION Muscular tubercle on base of skull

INNERVATION Ventral branch of local spinal nerve

FUNCTION Flexes/bends head laterally

DEVELOPMENT ISSUES Head unlevel, neck tight and stiff; horse does not take contact on affected side; head shaking or unsteady

RECTUS CAPITUS VENTRALIS (Figure 4.9)

ORIGIN Ventral arch of atlas

INSERTION Base of skull

INNERVATION Ventral branch of local spinal nerve

FUNCTION Flexes atlanto-occipital joint

DEVELOPMENT ISSUES As above

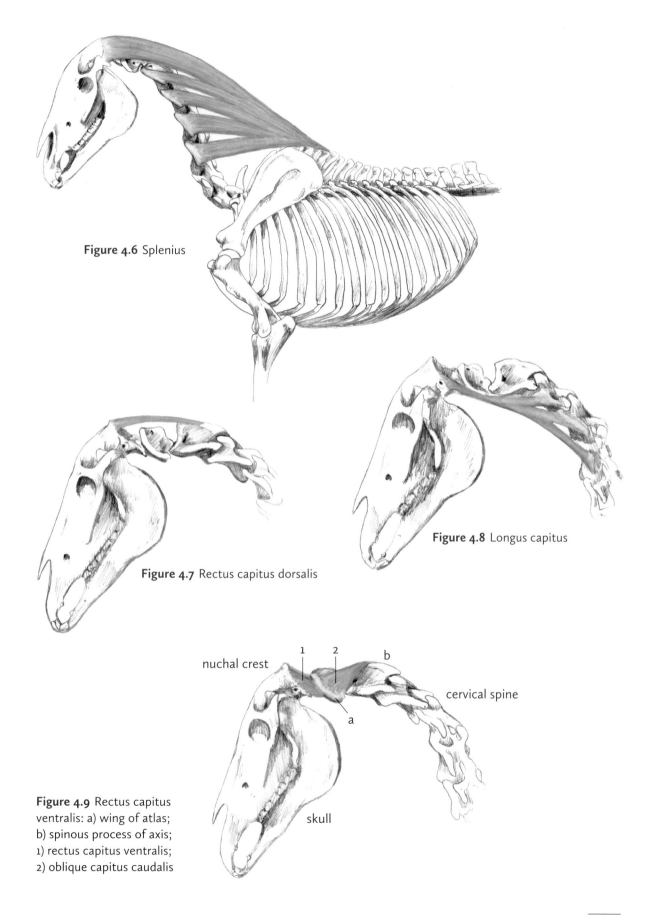

Figure 4.6 Splenius

Figure 4.7 Rectus capitus dorsalis

Figure 4.8 Longus capitus

nuchal crest

1   2   b

a

cervical spine

skull

Figure 4.9 Rectus capitus
ventralis: a) wing of atlas;
b) spinous process of axis;
1) rectus capitus ventralis;
2) oblique capitus caudalis

Atlanto-axial joint

In axial rotation the atlanto-axial joint has by far the greatest amount of movement. As this allows shaking of the head, it is also called the 'no' joint. In lateral bending the atlanto-occipital joint has a reasonably good range of movement but the atlanto-axial joint has barely any. This joint is acted upon mainly by the oblique capitus caudalis, sternocephalicus, and cleidomastoideus (part of brachiocephalic).

OBLIQUE CAPITUS CAUDALIS (Figure 4.9)

ORIGIN Spinous process of axis

INSERTION Wing of atlas

INNERVATION Dorsal branch C2

FUNCTION Rotates atlas (and head)

DEVELOPMENT ISSUES Horse reluctant to make lateral flexion

STERNOCEPHALICUS (Figure 4.10)

ORIGIN Manubrium of sternum and cariniform cartilage

INSERTION Mandible; caudal border of ramus

INNERVATION Accessory nerve ventral branch

FUNCTION Flexes/inclines head and neck

DEVELOPMENT ISSUES Hypertrophied; horse takes pull; lack of control

BRIACHIOCEPHALIC: made up of cleidomastoideus muscle in cranial portion and cleidobrachialis muscle in caudal portion which are divided at the clavicular inscription (Figure 4.11)

ORIGIN Medial deltoid tuberosity

INSERTION Mastoid process of temporal bone; wing of atlas; nuchal crest

INNERVATION Accessory nerve ventral branch

FUNCTION Flexes and turns head (also acts as forelimb protractor)

DEVELOPMENT ISSUES Unlevel gait in front, worse on circles; horse refusing to go forwards, with choppy stride

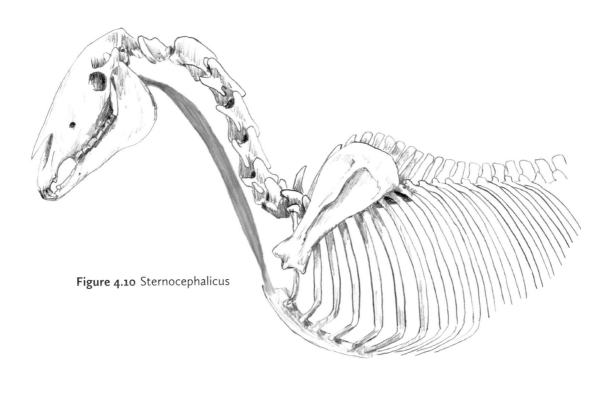

Figure 4.10 Sternocephalicus

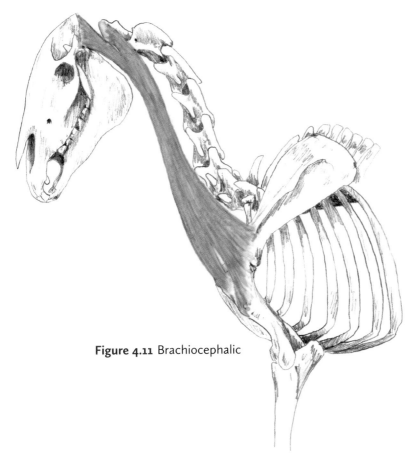

Figure 4.11 Brachiocephalic

This complete difference in each joint's range of movement (ROM), make it diagnostically significant. For example, if your horse has difficulty flexing at the poll, he may have a problem with the atlanto-occipital joint or the muscles responsible for its action. On the other hand, if he carries his head with a tilt, he may have a problem with the atlanto-axial joint or the muscles responsible for its action. If he has difficulty flexing to the left or right, he may well have a problem with the atlanto-occipital joint and muscles of action, but you can virtually rule out the atlanto-axial joint.

Axial rotation of the neck is mainly provided by the cervical portions of the **multifidus** muscle which also stabilises the neck.

MULTIFIDUS CERVICALIS (Figure 4.12)

ORIGIN Articular processes of last 6 cervical vertebrae

INSERTION Spinous process of preceding vertebra

INNERVATION Dorsal branch of local spinal nerve

FUNCTION Rotates head to opposite side of flexion; extends neck and flexes to side of contraction

DEVELOPMENT ISSUES Resistance in neck action, horse has poor contact with bit

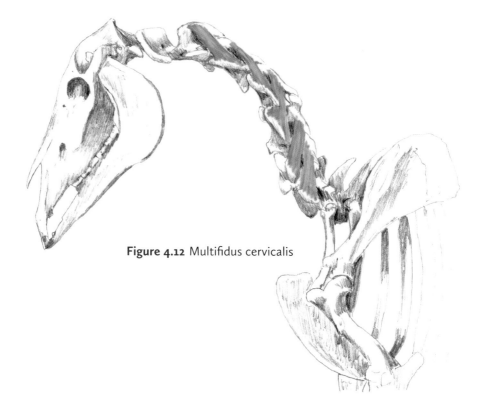

Figure 4.12 Multifidus cervicalis

The rest of the intervertebral joints in the horse's neck are fairly mobile and the transverse processes of C1–C6 can usually be palpated. C7 cannot be palpated because it is in between the shoulders. General movement of the neck is governed by the **longissimus (cervicalis), spinalis, iliocostalis, sternocephalic** (see above), **semispinalis capitus** and **cleidomastoideus** (see above) muscles.

LONGISSIMUS (Figure 4.13)

ORIGIN Transverse spinous processes of cervical vertebrae

INSERTION Wing of atlas; mastoid process of temporal bone

INNERVATION Dorsal branch of local spinal nerve

FUNCTION Elevates or bends head and neck laterally

DEVELOPMENT ISSUES Horse tilts head; poor contact in one rein

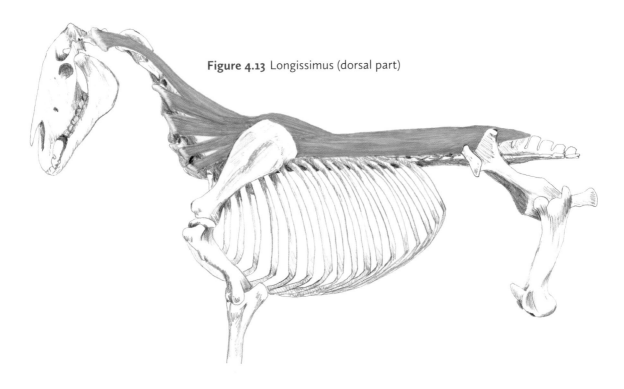

Figure 4.13 Longissimus (dorsal part)

SPINALIS (Figure 4.14)

ORIGIN Spinous processes of lumbar and last 6 thoracic vertebrae

INSERTION Spinous processes of first 6–7 thoracic and last 5 cervical vertebrae

INNERVATION Dorsal branch of local spinal nerve

FUNCTION Stabilises back and neck. Elevates neck or flexes laterally

DEVELOPMENT ISSUES Inability to flex neck to one side

ILIOCOSTALIS (Figure 4.15)

ORIGIN/INSERTION Between transverse spinous processes of C4 and T1 and first rib

INNERVATION Dorsal branch of local spinal nerve

FUNCTION Extends and flexes (laterally) neck

DEVELOPMENT ISSUES Inability to flex neck to one side

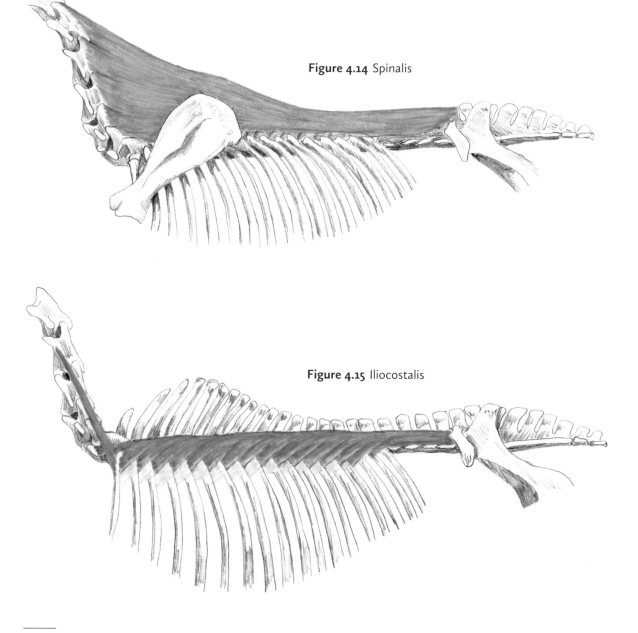

Figure 4.14 Spinalis

Figure 4.15 Iliocostalis

SEMISPINALIS CAPITUS (Figure 4.16)

ORIGIN Transverse spinous processes of first 6 thoracic vertebrae; articular processes of last 6 cervical vertebrae

INSERTION Occipital bone

INNERVATION Dorsal branch of local spinal nerve

FUNCTION Elevates head and neck; flexes neck laterally

DEVELOPMENT ISSUES General stiffness in horse's neck giving the rider a 'wooden' feel

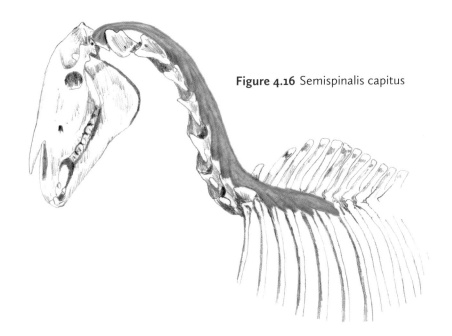

Figure 4.16 Semispinalis capitus

The neck in the horse is elongated not only to enable grazing (Figure 4.17) but it also plays a large part in movement and breathing, particularly at the faster gaits and when jumping. At these times the horse will raise and lower the head and neck set, using it like a pendulum, which affects the balance throughout the body.

When the neck is lifted up it then throws the weight to the back of the horse making it easier to lift the front end. Conversely when the neck is lowered, the weight is transferred to the front of the horse and makes the back end easier to lift up.

When you watch a racehorse in full gallop you can see this movement in the head and neck set. The head comes up when the horse needs to lift the front limbs, and the head goes down when he needs to lift the hind limbs.

Figure 4.17 The horse's elongated neck enables grazing. (Courtesy of Equine Articulated Skeletons Inc.)

Figure 4.18 The piston-pendulum effect. The horse lifts his head and neck (left) which enables him to lift the forehand and take a breath. When he lowers his head (right) it enables the hind end to be lifted and the compression of the viscera against the diaphragm forces exhalation.

Very cleverly this system also regulates the horse's breathing in the canter and gallop, in what is known as the 'piston-pendulum' effect. When the horse's head goes down and the non-lead forelimb hits the ground, it exerts a decelerative force, but the weight of the viscera keeps moving forwards (like the passengers in a car when the driver slams on the brakes) and compresses the diaphragm, forcing the horse to exhale. When the head comes up, the viscera slide backwards, forcing the horse to inhale. This is another energy saving system in the prey animal because no energy is wasted on muscles being used for respiration.

Figure 4.18 represents both the movement and the respiratory effects of neck raising and lowering very clearly. The neck thus plays an extremely important part in equine locomotion and should therefore be kept in the best condition possible.

Shoulder region

For the purposes of this book the shoulder region is that between T1 and T11. Although this is a completely arbitrary definition in terms of anatomy, the function of this section needs to be appreciated in order to understand its part in overall movement. Indeed ROM in the shoulder region is vitally important for the athletic horse, because not only does it attach the front limb to the body of the horse, the ventral (chest) muscles support the forehand.

The horse, unlike bipeds such as humans, does not have a clavicle and therefore there is no bony joint between the front limb and the body of the horse, which would equate to our shoulder joint. In the horse (as in most of the veterinary mammals) the scapula is 'strapped' to the thorax by means of muscles and other soft tissues. The muscles which perform this function are called the **extrinsic muscles of the shoulder**. These extrinsic muscles are mainly the **trapezius, omotransversarius, rhomboideus,** and **latissimus dorsi**.

TRAPEZIUS (Figure 4.19)

ORIGIN Nuchal and supraspinous ligaments from C2 to T10

INSERTION Thoracic portion: dorsal third of scapular spine; cervical portion: entire scapular spine

INNERVATION Dorsal branch of accessory nerve

FUNCTION Elevates scapula, and can move scapula craniodorsally and caudodorsally

DEVELOPMENT ISSUES Underdevelopment noted as dip in front of withers; poor shoulder movement, lack of co-ordination and short choppy cranial phase of forelimb stride

OMOTRANSVERSARIUS (Figure 4.20)

ORIGIN Shoulder fascia/scapula spine

INSERTION Transverse spinous processes of C2–4

INNERVATION Medioventral branch of local cervical nerve

FUNCTION Protracts limb when neck fixed; flexes neck when limb fixed

DEVELOPMENT ISSUES Gait unlevel in front; fused ventrally with cleidomastoideus

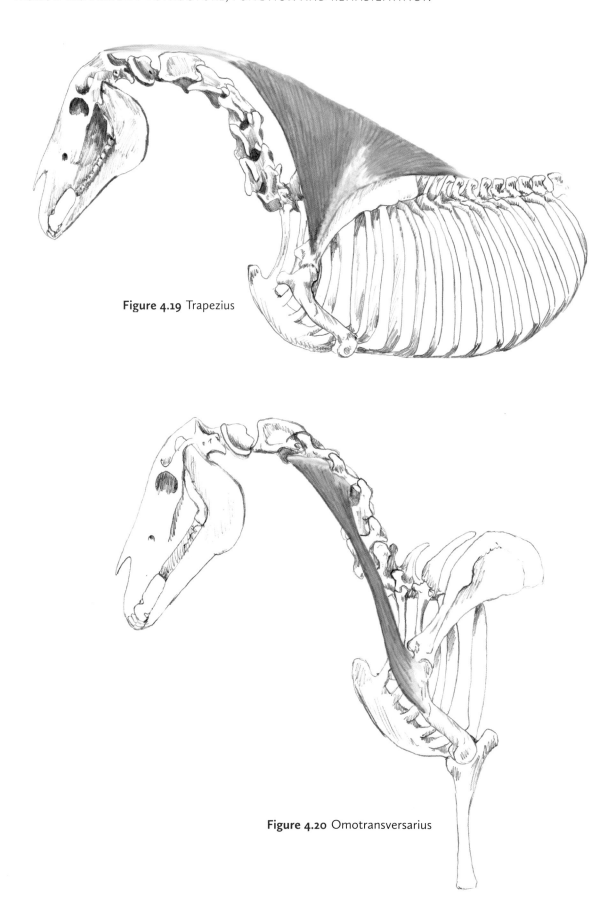

Figure 4.19 Trapezius

Figure 4.20 Omotransversarius

RHOMBOIDEUS (Figure 4.21)

ORIGIN Nuchal and dorsoscapular ligaments from C2 to T8

INSERTION Scapular cartilage

INNERVATION Medioventral branch of local thoracic and cervical nerve

FUNCTION Moves scapula dorsally and cranially; elevates shoulder

DEVELOPMENT ISSUES Poor shoulder activity; affects co-ordination of front limbs

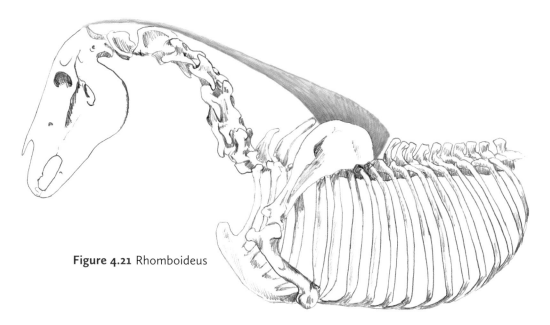

Figure 4.21 Rhomboideus

LATISSIMUS DORSI (Figure 4.22)

ORIGIN Supraspinous ligament from T3 caudally via thoracolumbar fascia

INSERTION Teres major tuberosity of humerus together with teres major muscle

INNERVATION Thoracodorsal nerve

FUNCTION Retracts limb; flexes shoulder joint; when limb fixes draws trunk cranially

DEVELOPMENT ISSUES General forehand stiffness seen predominantly on circles; gives wooden feel to rider

However, here must be mentioned a very large muscle that supports the weight of the neck and thorax of the horse from its attachment on the inside of the shoulder blade: the **serratus ventralis**.

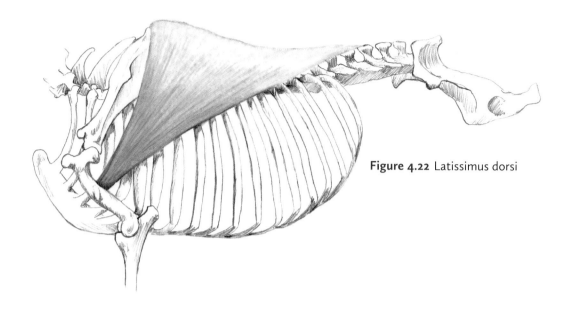

Figure 4.22 Latissimus dorsi

SERRATUS VENTRALIS (Figure 4.23)

ORIGIN Transverse spinous processes of C4–7; lateral surfaces of 1st–8th ribs (inserted with tendinous sheaths)

INSERTION Scapular cartilage medial aspect of scapula

INNERVATION Ventral branch of local spinal nerves; long thoracic nerve

FUNCTION Lifts body in relation to scapula, suspends trunk between scapulae.

DEVELOPMENT ISSUES General forehand stiffness seen predominantly on circles; can be noted to hold trunk in a tilted position if one side is hypertonic

This is the major part of what is known as a 'synsarcotic' connection, which simply means that it is a joint formed of soft tissues. The extrinsic muscles of the shoulder together with the serratus ventralis support nearly all the weight of the thorax, and as 60 per cent of a horse's weight is taken on the front limbs then these soft tissues have to be in the best possible condition. They are also responsible for much of the forelimb movement in all planes, so you can begin to understand the importance of this shoulder movement in correct movement and athletic ability.

The structure of the vertebrae in this shoulder area reflects the power and need for support for these muscles to act against the skeleton for support and movement. These thoracic vertebrae have extremely long dorsal spinous processes (DSPs) and these can clearly be seen in the illustration of the axial skeleton at the beginning of this chapter (see Figure 4.1). On the surface anatomy these thoracic vertebrae represent the basis of the withers (Photo 4.24).

However, the ventral muscles of this portion of the body, which lie between the horse's front legs, also play a huge part in the support of the thorax and in movement. These are the pectoral group of muscles which comprise the **subclavius, deep pectoral, transverse pectoral,** and **superficial pectoral** muscles.

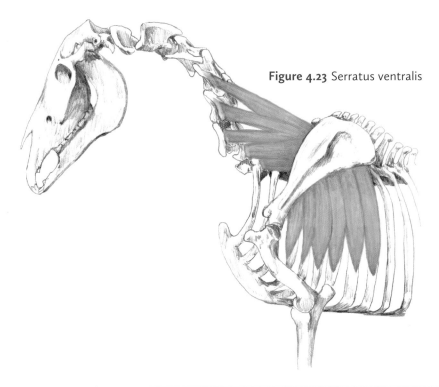

Figure 4.23 Serratus ventralis

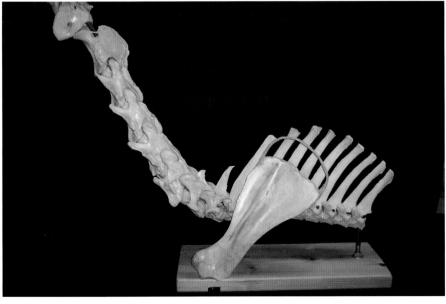

Photo 4.24 The neck vertebrae and the thoracic vertebrae which comprise the shoulder region (T1–T11). (Courtesy of Equine Articulated Skeletons Inc.)

SUBCLAVIUS (Figure 4.25)

ORIGIN Sternum and costal cartilages 1–4

INSERTION Supraspinatus and shoulder fascia

INNERVATION Cranial pectoral nerve

FUNCTION Suspends trunk and stabilises shoulder

DEVELOPMENT ISSUES General forehand stiffness and incoordination

DEEP PECTORAL (Figure 4.26)

ORIGIN Sternum; distally on ribs 4–9; abdominal fascia

INSERTION Major and minor tubercles of humerus; tendon of origin of coracobrachialis

INNERVATION Cranial and caudal pectoral nerve

FUNCTION Suspends trunk between forelimbs; retracts limb; stabilises shoulder

DEVELOPMENT ISSUES Short stride; inability to stretch over fence; reacts to tightening of girth

TRANSVERSE PECTORAL (Figure 4.27)

ORIGIN Costal cartilages 1–6 and adjacent sternum

INSERTION Forearm fascia

INNERVATION Cranial and caudal pectoral nerves

FUNCTION To connect forelimbs with trunk; adducts and resists abduction of forelimbs

DEVELOPMENT ISSUES Shortens stride and gives uncoordinated forelimb movement

SUPERFICIAL PECTORAL (Figure 4.27)

ORIGIN Manubrium sterni

INSERTION Deltoid tuberosity of humerus

INNERVATION Cranial and caudal pectoral nerves

FUNCTION Protracts and retracts forelimb

DEVELOPMENT ISSUES Short stride

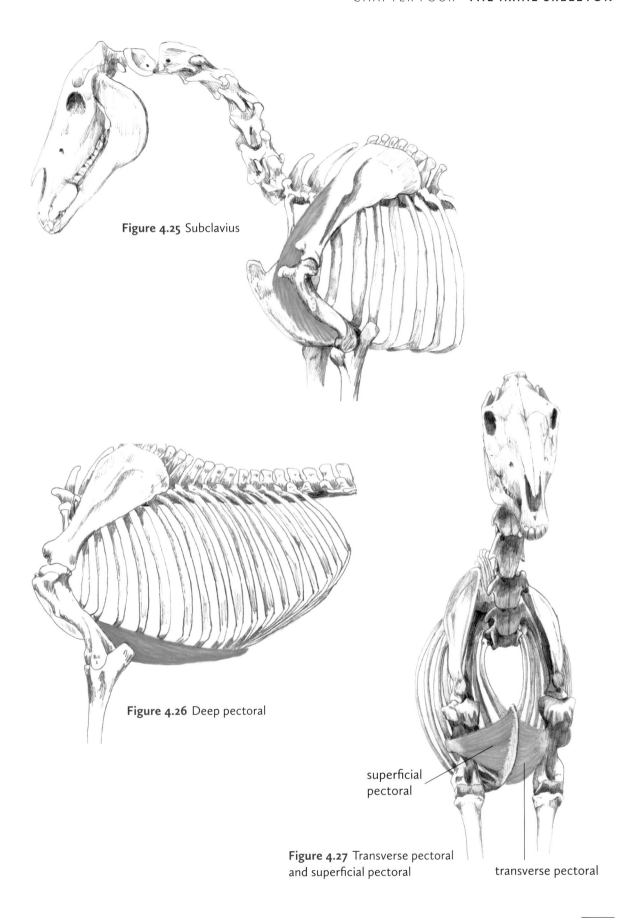

Figure 4.25 Subclavius

Figure 4.26 Deep pectoral

superficial
pectoral

Figure 4.27 Transverse pectoral
and superficial pectoral

transverse pectoral

The H frame

Figure 4.28
below Diagrammatic
representation of the
body of the horse
suspended between
the shoulder blades
(scapulae) and
supported by the
pectoral group, as
viewed from the
front of the horse.

Functionally it can be imagined that the front legs, the shoulder blades, the pectorals, the extrinsic shoulder muscles and the serratus ventralis act like an H frame with the thorax suspended between the two top uprights of the H (Figure 4.28).

This functional arrangement endows the horse with many movement and athletic benefits. For example, it allows the thorax to swing between the scapulae by abducting (moving away) and adducting (bringing towards) each front limb (Figures 4.29a and b). The body of the horse can therefore 'swing in the cradle' of the scapulae to enable him to bend around corners and work on a circle.

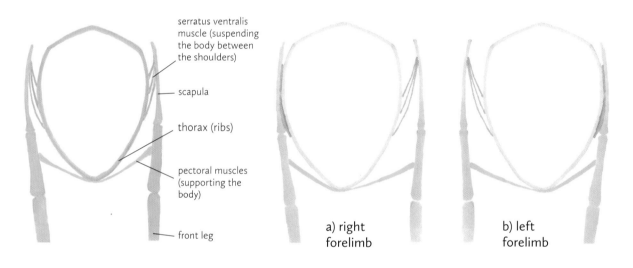

serratus ventralis muscle (suspending the body between the shoulders)

scapula

thorax (ribs)

pectoral muscles (supporting the body)

front leg

a) right forelimb

b) left forelimb

Figures 4.29a and b
above right Looking
from the front of the
horse: a) right forelimb
drawn towards the
thorax; b) left forelimb
drawn towards the
thorax.

Inability to bend through the body

If you review the ROM of the thoracic vertebrae in the shoulders it can be seen that there is very little, if any, lateral movement in this area. Indeed, that is of necessity because the forelimbs have to be anchored to a stable structure. We have all seen the classic drawing in equitation texts apparently demonstrating that the horse can bend equally from poll to tail when on a circle (Figure 4.30). Unfortunately this is nonsense; we know from our studies of anatomy that there is very little bending behind the saddle and, indeed, the sacral vertebrae are fused together and cannot flex.

So how did we become so confused about this apparently vital, but completely impossible, function of the equine spinal column? How can the horse appear to bend equally around the rider's inside leg, when we know that he cannot?

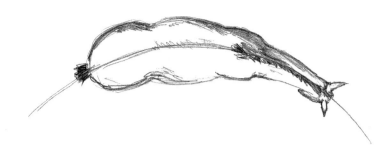

Figure 4.30 A completely erroneous illustration of a horse 'bending' throughout the length of his body. This is anatomically impossible.

The answer is the aforementioned 'swinging in the cradle' function of the back. The neck can bend as seen in the diagram but, as we found out in this section, there is little movement in the shoulder area. The apparent 'bend' is caused by the horse drawing the inside forelimb towards his thorax (adducting) but moving the outside forelimb away from the thorax (abducting).

Scapular movement

One further important aspect of the shoulder area is known as 'scapular glide'. We have seen that the scapulae are strapped to the sides of the body of the horse by soft tissue structures rather than with a bony joint. This allows the scapula to move and rotate against the thorax.

Figure 4.31 shows an image taken from computer-aided gait-analysis images. An appreciation of the shoulder movement can be gained from this image, and throughout the small amount of stride phase that is illustrated, the scapula has not only moved backwards and forwards but it has rotated slightly. Bear in mind that this is just at an in-hand trot speed and that the faster the gait the greater the shoulder movement has to be to accommodate the larger stride lengths that need to be achieved. Therefore a greater shoulder movement is positively correlated with longer strides, so the more supple and free the shoulder, the greater the limb protraction and retraction. Speed and extended gaits are, therefore, very much affected by shoulder movement.

Folding of the forelimbs

Jumping is another athletic activity which needs maximum shoulder movement. When the horse flexes his forelimbs to negotiate the top rail, the complete 'folding' of the limbs has a great dependence on shoulder joint flexion. That shoulder flexion is enhanced by the scapula rotating

Figure 4.31 *right*
Computerised gait-analysis system demonstrating scapular movement. (Courtesy of Russell Guire, Centaur Biomechanics)

Figure 4.32 *below*
Skeletal representation of jumping action. (Courtesy of Equine Articulated Skeletons Inc.)

backwards. In Figure 4.32 we see the skeletal reproduction of the horse jumping, and how the front legs need to fold up to clear the fence.

However, in the elite jumping horse, that limb folding function has to work to extremes, and therefore the shoulder flexibility becomes of paramount importance. As an example have a look at Photos 4.33a and b, which show Sarah Stretton and Lazy Acres Skip On negotiating the Burghley show-jumping and cross-country courses.

By making a comparison between the front limb folding of the jumping skeleton and that of Skip On, it is clear that the elite jumping horse has to make extreme use of the shoulder movement. Because of the soft tissue nature of shoulder attachment to the body, this is something that equine sports physiotherapists can enhance considerably.

The more that the horse can wind up those front limbs, the less of a jumping effort he has to make, and the less energy he has to expend in the jumping effort. If the front limbs were dangling in any way, he would have to jump much higher to clear the fence and that would expend a lot more energy.

Photos 4.33a and b
above and left
Note how the forelimbs of the horse are wound up tightly so that they clear the back rail of the show jump and the cross-country fence. This requires exceptional shoulder freedom.

We can therefore take from this that free and unencumbered movement of the shoulder is vital to sustain fluid movement and athletic ability. Dressage horses are, in part, selected for freedom of the shoulder. In Photo 4.34 we see a quite extraordinary shoulder movement in a yearling colt by Totilas. The scapula has rotated to allow forelimb protraction.

One way of checking that the shoulder is free is to see if you can get your fingers between the front of the scapula and the thorax (Photo 4.35). Generally, the horse with shoulder freedom will find this enjoyable and relaxing.

Photo 4.34 Note the extraordinary shoulder rotation in this young warmblood. (Courtesy of Catherine Gallegos)

Photo 4.35 Freedom of the shoulder can be detected by easily getting fingers in between the shoulder blade and thorax.

Clearly, if shoulder movement is such an important part of movement and athleticism, then anything that would impede shoulder movement should be avoided. The most likely cause of shoulder impingement is a poorly fitting saddle, and this will be discussed later on in this book.

Mid-back and lumbar region (the thoracolumbar bow)

As with the shoulder region, the section that comprises this region, from T12 to T18 (mid-back) and L1 to L6, is purely arbitrary and its selection is based on biomechanics rather than on anatomy. Indeed the anatomical differences between the structure of the thoracic vertebrae and the lumbar vertebrae are marked.

It is in the mid-back section that the second most intervertebral joint movement is possible (after the neck), particularly in lateral flexion. However, it also just happens to be the part of the back upon which the saddle and rider sit. Clearly therefore, any interference in back movement during riding is going to have a marked effect upon the mechanics of this mid-back area. It will thus come as no surprise that poor saddle fit and a leaden rider are the likely culprits in mid-back movement restriction.

It is also this part of the back that has to support the weight of the saddle and rider and, again, the mechanics by which this is achieved by the horse is unique.

If you sit on the middle of a rectangular table with a leg at each corner, then not only will the table bend in the middle but the legs will splay out in front and behind (Figure 4.36).

It would be unfortunate if we sat on the horse and his legs shot out in front and behind him. But not only can he resist these forces, he can also

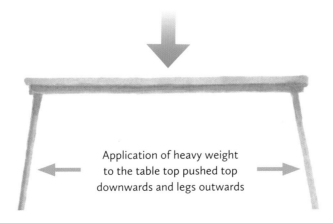

Application of heavy weight to the table top pushed top downwards and legs outwards

Figure 4.36 The application of heavy weight to a table top will push the top downwards and the legs outwards.

gallop at full speed and jump with a rider and tack on his back. This is especially ingenious when you consider how thin and light his lower limbs are, compared to the weight and muscularity of his back.

So how does the horse achieve this? By the mechanical analogue for the horse's back known as the 'bow and string theory'.

The bow and string theory

Imagine using a longbow, like the type that Robin Hood used (Figure 4.37); when you tighten the string the bow flexes (arches more) and when you loosen the string the bow flattens out.

So now try thinking of the bow as the horse's back (dorsal line) and the string as his abdominal muscles (ventral line), particularly the rectus abdominus muscle (Figure 4.38).

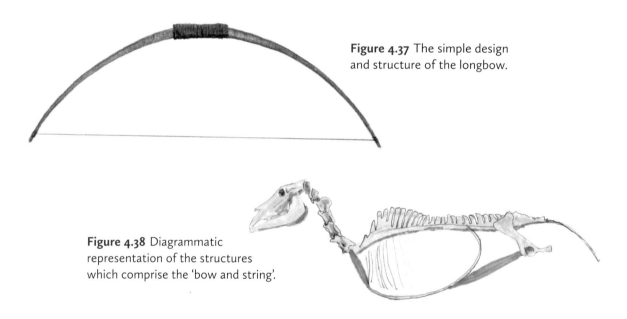

Figure 4.37 The simple design and structure of the longbow.

Figure 4.38 Diagrammatic representation of the structures which comprise the 'bow and string'.

RECTUS ABDOMINUS (Figure 4.39)

ORIGIN Lateral surface of costal cartilages 4–9

INSERTION Prebubic tendon and (via accessory ligament) on head of femur

INNERVATION Local intercostal and ventral branches of lumbar nerves

FUNCTION Flexes lumbar spine and lumbosacral joint

DEVELOPMENT ISSUES Inability to bring hind limb sufficiently underneath to support rider and go forwards

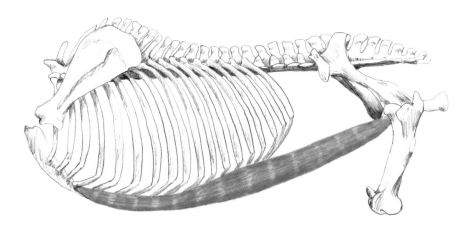

Figure 4.39 Rectus abdominus

EXTERNAL ABDOMINAL OBLIQUE (Figure 4.40)

ORIGIN Lateral surface of ribs 4–18; thoracolumbar fascia

INSERTION Abdominal tendon: linea alba and prepubic tendon; pelvic tendon: tuber coxae and prepubic tendon

INNERVATION Local intercostal and ventral branches of lumbar nerves

FUNCTION Flexes the trunk

DEVELOPMENT ISSUES Inability to bring hind limb sufficiently underneath to support rider and go forwards

INTERNAL ABDOMINAL OBLIQUE (Figure 4.41)

ORIGIN Tuber coxae and adjacent inguinal ligament

INSERTION Last rib; cartilages of last 5 ribs, linea alba and prepubic tendon

INNERVATION Local intercostal and ventral branches of lumbar nerves

FUNCTION Flexes the trunk

DEVELOPMENT ISSUES As above

TRANSVERSE ABDOMINUS (Figure 4.42)

ORIGIN Medial surface of costal cartilages 7–18; lumbar transverse processes

INSERTION Linea alba

INNERVATION Local intercostal and ventral branches of lumbar nerves

FUNCTION Flexes the trunk

DEVELOPMENT ISSUES As above

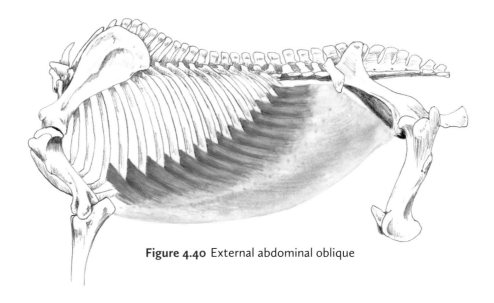

Figure 4.40 External abdominal oblique

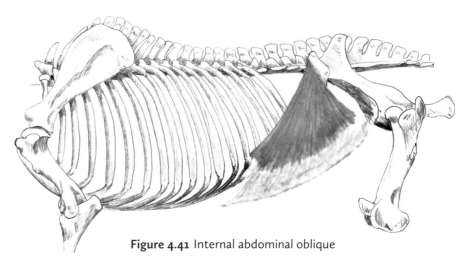

Figure 4.41 Internal abdominal oblique

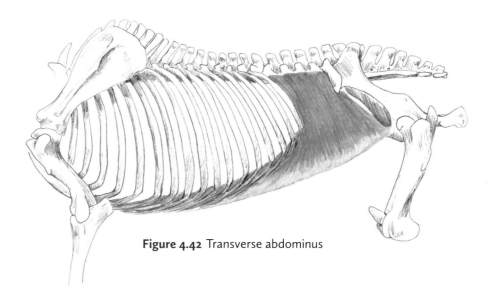

Figure 4.42 Transverse abdominus

When the horse contracts the rectus abdominus (and other abdominal muscles), it pulls the pelvis closer to the sternum and changes the angle of the lumbosacral joint, just like the string of the bow pulling the two ends together. This effectively shortens the ventral line (the underline) of the horse and at the same time the dorsal line (the topline) must lengthen and flex, and the hind limb can be placed further underneath the horse.

LONGISSIMUS (See Figure 4.13)

ORIGIN Spinous processes of sacrum, lumbar and thoracic vertebrae; wing of ilium; transverse processes of thoracic and cervical vertebrae

INSERTION Transverse spinous processes of vertebrae; tubercles of ribs; wing of atlas; and mastoid process of temporal bone

INNERVATION Dorsal branch of local spinal nerves

FUNCTION Stabilises and extends vertebral column; elevates or bends head laterally

DEVELOPMENT ISSUES Sore, tight neck and/or back, giving rider a stiff and wooden feel; reluctance to engage and go forwards

SPINALIS (See Figure 4.14)

ORIGIN Spinous processes of lumbar and last 6 thoracic vertebrae

INSERTION Spinous processes of first 6 thoracic and last 5 cervical vertebrae

INNERVATION Dorsal branch of local spinal nerves

FUNCTION Stabilises back and neck; elevates neck or bends it laterally

DEVELOPMENT ISSUES As above

MULTIFIDUS (Figure 4.43)

ORIGIN Articular and mammillary processes of all vertebrae from C2 to sacrum

INSERTION Spinous processes of preceding vertebrae

INNERVATION Dorsal branch of local spinal nerves

FUNCTION Stabilises and twists the vertebral column

DEVELOPMENT ISSUES As above

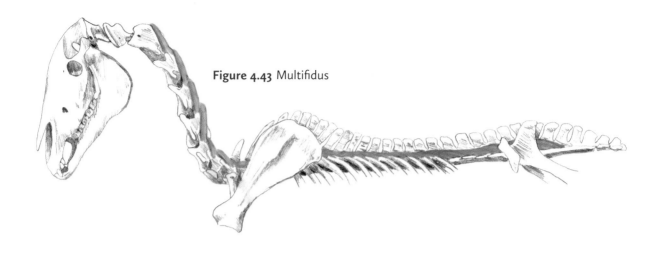

Figure 4.43 Multifidus

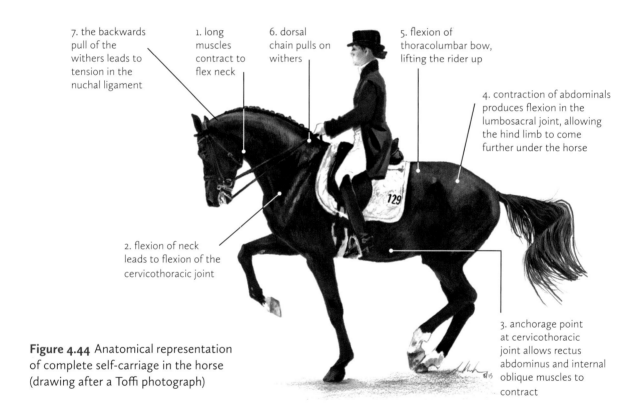

7. the backwards pull of the withers leads to tension in the nuchal ligament

1. long muscles contract to flex neck

6. dorsal chain pulls on withers

5. flexion of thoracolumbar bow, lifting the rider up

4. contraction of abdominals produces flexion in the lumbosacral joint, allowing the hind limb to come further under the horse

2. flexion of neck leads to flexion of the cervicothoracic joint

3. anchorage point at cervicothoracic joint allows rectus abdominus and internal oblique muscles to contract

Figure 4.44 Anatomical representation of complete self-carriage in the horse (drawing after a Toffi photograph)

As the back lengthens and flexes, the dorsal spinous processes of the vertebrae in the shoulder and thoracolumbar bow open up and exert a backwards pull on the withers, which lifts the forehand. At the same time the scalenus muscle which connects the first rib to the cervicothoracic joint contracts and this enables the head and neck set to elevate, and the horse to work forwards in complete self-carriage. It is this anatomical function that gives the rider the glorious feeling of being lifted up and floated forwards as represented in Figure 4.44.

This then leads us to the concept of dorsal (topline) and ventral (underline) muscular chains. When looking at Figure 4.44 it can be appreciated that to perform in this perfect self-carriage, the horse has to make the dorsal chain (extending from the poll to the back of the stifles) as long as possible whilst making the ventral chain (extending from the throat, along the abdominals and ending at the insertion of the rectus abdominus onto the pelvis) as short as possible. However, just like any chain, it is only as strong as its weakest link, and it only takes one muscle within this whole process to be injured or painful, and the whole self-carriage concept will fail.

When training the young horse, or when rehabilitating a horse after injury, there is only one ultimate goal and that is to train for this balance of dorsal and ventral chains, as this will form the complete postural and biomechanical base from which you can begin to build/rebuild the athlete. So whilst this abdominal suppleness is being achieved, the young or damaged horse should be worked in the position we know as 'long and low' when the head is lower than the withers and the neck is reaching out and down so that the length between the poll and the back of the stifles is as long as you can make it. Establishing this correct posture from the beginning will also have a profound effect on your horse's weight carrying and athletic ability.

If this system fails to function because, for example, the long muscles in the back are sore or in spasm and cannot lengthen, then this is the start of a potentially long downward spiral into poor posture, loss of performance and behavioural changes due to pain. The effects of this will be demonstrated in Chapter 5, and schooling strategies to rehabilitate following these effects will be discussed in Chapter 8.

Energy saving

At this stage it is necessary to discuss another function of the lumbar vertebrae. You can see from the graphs at the beginning of this chapter that there is hardly any intervertebral joint movement in the lumbar region of the horse and, again, the reason for this is rooted in the evolution of the horse as a prey animal.

The horse's major means of defence is to outrun a predator. Therefore as much energy as possible has to be put into the systems that propel him forwards and away from whatever is chasing him. Any energy that is used for body movements not associated with forward propulsion is wasted energy.

The principles of elastic energy were discussed in Chapter 1, but this energy-saving system needs more than elastic energy. When you look at a horse walking, you are looking for a nice fluid action through the back, with the quarters swaying from side to side. But swaying from side to side wastes energy that could more usefully be spent on propelling the horse forwards and away from the predator.

The reason why the vertebrae behind the saddle in the horse do not allow much movement is that they are designed to act as a mechanical strut against which the hind limbs can exert the power created by hind limb retractor muscles. This ensures that all the power generated to propel the horse forwards is not wasted in any other type of movement. Therefore, as the horse's gaits get faster he loses the sideways sway in the back that is seen in the walk, and if you watch racehorses from behind on the gallops, you will see that there is absolutely no sideways motion at all, every ounce of energy is being used to drive the horse forwards.

Lumbosacral joint

In Figure 4.3 it can be seen that normal movement in the lumbosacral joint is about 30 degrees in the flexion and extension planes. We have demonstrated that lumbosacral joint flexion and extension is vital in correct movement. Therefore, the greater amount of movement in the lumbosacral joint, the more the angle of the pelvis can change and the greater the athletic ability. This is because the more flexion in the lumbosacral joint, the more the horse can bring the hind leg underneath him and this is important for speed, jumping, and extended and collected movements. In changing the angle of the lumbosacral joint, as the 'string' shortens, the back lifts and flexes and the dorsal and ventral muscular chains function in harmony.

Also the further underneath him the horse can place his hind limb, the longer the stance phase (when the foot is on the ground). Greater stance time equals greater propulsion forwards (for speed) and upwards (for jumping). It is also vital for collected movements in dressage as the hind limb must come well under the body. Take a look at Photos 4.45 and 4.46 and compare the angle of the hind limb in the first picture with the hind limb angle in the second. A lot of this difference in angle comes from lumbo-sacral joint movement. Bringing the hind limb underneath (limb protraction) is a function of lumbosacral joint flexibility, suppleness in the back muscles and the elastic energy released by the ilipsoas muscle causing protraction of the hind limb (see Fig.1.2 in Chapter 1). It also requires the part of the dorsal muscular chain between the lumbosacral joint and the back of the stifles (the hamstring group – see chart on page 96 and illustrations on pages 46 and 47 Chapter 3) to be able to lengthen and contract to the maximum.

Photo 4.45 The horse's hind limb in maximum protraction.

Photo 4.46 The horse's hind limb in full retraction (courtesy of Nico Morgan).

BICEPS FEMORIS (See Figure 3.6)

ORIGIN a. Vertebral head: spinous and transverse processes of last three sacral vertebrae, sacrosciatic ligament and tail fascia; b. pelvic head: tuber ischia

INSERTION a. Patella, lateral and middle patella ligaments; b. cranial border of tibia and crural fascia; c. via long calcanean tendon to calcaneus

INNERVATION Caudal gluteal and sciatic nerves

FUNCTION a. Extends hip and stifle; b. with caudal division flexes stifle; c. abducts hind limb

DEVELOPMENT ISSUES Shortening of cranial portion of stride; resists lateral movement; discomfort in hind joints

SEMITENDINOSUS (See Figure 3.7)

ORIGIN a. Vertebral head: last sacral and first two caudal vertebrae, tail fascia and sacrosciatic ligament; b. pelvic head: ventral tuber ischia

INSERTION a. Cranial border of tibia, crural fascia; b. via long calcanean tendon to calcanius

INNERVATION Caudal gluteal and sciatic nerves

FUNCTION a. During weight bearing: extends hip, stifle and hock; b. during non-weight bearing: retracts and adducts limb

DEVELOPMENT ISSUES As above

SEMIMEMBRANOSUS (See Figure 3.8)

ORIGIN a. Vertebral head: first caudal vertebra, sacrosciatic ligament; b. pelvic head: ventromedial aspect of tuber ischia

INSERTION Medial condyles of femur and tibia

INNERVATION Caudal gluteal and sciatic nerves

FUNCTION a. During weight bearing: extends hip and stifle; b. during non-weight bearing: retracts and adducts limb

DEVELOPMENT ISSUES As above

Once the hind limb is on the ground, the powerful action of the gluteal and hamstring groups retract the hind limb, and again, change the angle of the pelvis to propel the horse forwards and/or upwards (see chart opposite and illustrations on page 44 of Chapter 3)

MIDDLE GLUTEAL (See Figure 3.3)

ORIGIN a. Longissimus lumborum; b. gluteal surface of ilium; c. sacrum; d. sacroiliac and sacrosciatic ligaments

INSERTION Greater trochanter at head of femur

INNERVATION Cranial gluteal nerve

FUNCTION a. Extends hip; b. abducts hind limb

DEVELOPMENT ISSUES Reduced step length; resists lateral movement

DEEP GLUTEAL (See Figure 3.5)

ORIGIN Spine of ischia

INSERTION Greater trochanter at head of femur

INNERVATION Cranial gluteal nerve

FUNCTION Abducts hind limb

DEVELOPMENT ISSUES As above

Unfortunately it is the very same combination of unencumbered neck movement, balance of dorsal and ventral muscular chains and exceptional lumbosacral movement that allows the extremely athletic horse to buck very extravagantly!

Congratulations go to Team GB rider Sarah Stretton for staying on-board as Lazy Acres Skip On decides to prove the point in the warm-up arena (Photos 4.47a and b).

Photos 4.47a and b
Skip On makes full use of his neck, shortening of his ventral line and his gluteal and hamstrings muscle groups to make Sarah's position extremely precarious.

The functioning of the equine axial skeleton is, therefore, of prime importance in keeping a horse sound and at full athletic performance. Because there is such a heavy reliance on muscular function throughout, very careful consideration must be given to its development right from the start of your conditioning programme. Also, as many of the structures are reliant on other structures in the system functioning properly, any injury or incorrect development affects the whole system and your horse will never reach his true athletic potential and will always be prone to injury.

CHAPTER FIVE

Functional Responses to Exercise and Injury:

The use of thermal imaging techniques

A<small>LL MAMMALIAN MOVEMENT</small> stems from the soft tissues acting upon the skeleton, changing joint angles and stabilising the animal. The more effective the soft tissue function, the better the athletic performance. As soft tissues work, they heat up, not only because of the increased blood supply to the tissues, but also some of the elastic energy stored in the tissues is released as heat. This is why we 'warm-up' slowly, to enable the soft tissues to function at their optimum with the least possible chance of injury; the harder the tissue works, the greater the heat that builds up in that tissue.

If tissue is injured, however, then this evokes the body's inflammatory response, which is part of the complex biological response of vascular tissues to harmful stimuli, such as damaged cells, or irritants. The classic signs of acute inflammation are pain, heat, redness, swelling, and loss of function. Indeed, this is why the vet will look for heat in tissues when performing a lameness diagnosis, but in subtle injuries, heat produced by a minor inflammatory response may not be felt, or the structure that is damaged may be too deep to ascertain increases in temperature by palpation.

Visualisation of this process has recently become possible with the use of thermal imaging.

What is thermal imaging?

Thermal imaging can detect even subtle changes in heat in a tissue created by the inflammatory response. Thermal imaging is non-invasive, emits no radiation and can be repeated as frequently as required.

Thermal images are obtained by using a special camera that is effectively taking 'heat maps' rather than pictures. In Figure 5.1, which is a thermal image of both front pasterns and feet in a horse, obvious thermal differences are seen between the right and left distal limbs. Normally, thermal patterns will be symmetrical but clearly there is an inflammatory response in the left limb because of the redder patterns. Differences in heat can be measured from the scale on the right of the image. In this image the thermal image has picked up what turned out to be a subchondral bone cyst in the left pastern denoted by the red and white thermal pattern from increased heat produced by the body's inflammatory response.

Thermal imaging cameras are very sensitive to changes in the muscular, vascular, skeletal and nervous systems, detecting temperature differences of less than 0.05 °C, which is 40 times more sensitive than the human hand and can therefore detect inflammation in tissues which would not be evident upon palpation. So not only can it be used to detect injury and recovery, it can also measure the heat build-up in tissues as a result of exercise. In this way we can determine which muscles are working the hardest.

It can be very useful in pinpointing areas of interest for further investigation by the vet or physiotherapist and images are available immediately. Photo 5.2 shows Helen Morrell of Surrey Vet Physio discussing with the owner a thermal image she has just taken of the horse.

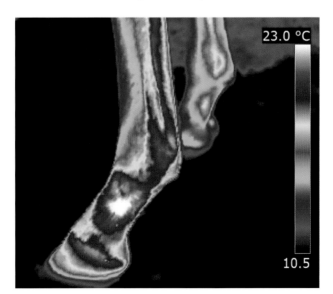

Figure 5.1 Subchondral bone cyst in the left pastern denoted by the white portion on the thermal image.

Photo 5.2 Thermal images can be discussed with the owner at the time of imaging.

Photo 5.3 *below left* Thermal images uploaded onto computer for digital transmission to a vet or physiotherapist together with the thermographer's interpretation of the images.

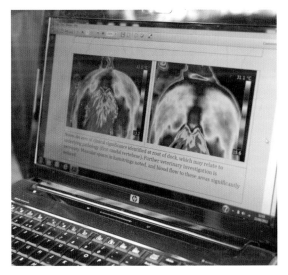

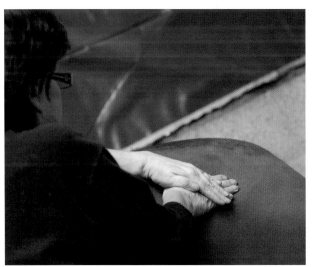

These images can be uploaded onto a computer screen (Photo 5.3) with the thermographer's interpretation which can be emailed to the vet or physiotherapist and can be used as a basis for further veterinary investigation or treatment choice, such as massage therapy (Photo 5.4).

Photo 5.4 *above right* A physiotherapist can use thermal imaging as a basis for selecting the appropriate treatment modality.

Thermal imaging as an aid to correct training

The use of thermal imaging can assist in the understanding and application of correct training principles when conditioning or rehabilitating a horse. Horses ridden and schooled correctly build up muscle symmetrically and in balance, with no tension or spasm, but horses allowed to run onto the forchand, for example, overuse the muscles at the base of the neck and at the shoulder. So how does that type of incorrect schooling reflect in the muscle build-up of the horse?

Figure 5.5 is a thermal image of a young horse being ridden incorrectly with the rider simply acting as a 'passenger' and failing to support or influence the movement of the horse, in much the same way as a beginner learning to ride would do. Effectively the horse is running onto the forehand. This image was taken after riding in this manner for 15 minutes (a typical warming-up session).

Bearing in mind that the 'engine' of the horse is in the quarters, it should be the muscles in that area which are the warmest. But in fact you can see that the warmest muscles (denoted by the red colours) are in the shoulder and the base of the neck, as the horse pulls himself along on the forehand, rather than pushing from behind.

After a suitable period of rest in which the muscles have been allowed to return to normal temperature, the same rider rides the horse for 15 minutes in a professional manner. In Figure 5.6 you see the startling difference in the way the horse's muscles are working. In this image the dorsal and ventral chains are working in harmony. Note the change of the angle of the pelvis from Figure 5.5 to Figure 5.6. The rectus abdominus muscle has pulled the pelvis closer to the sternum, opening up the lumbosacral joint and allowing the horse to bring the hind limb further underneath himself, radically rebalancing the horse.

Figure 5.5 Ineffective application of the rider's aids, so the horse is running onto the forehand. Note the red colours in the shoulder and base of the neck indicating this this horse is running on the forehand.

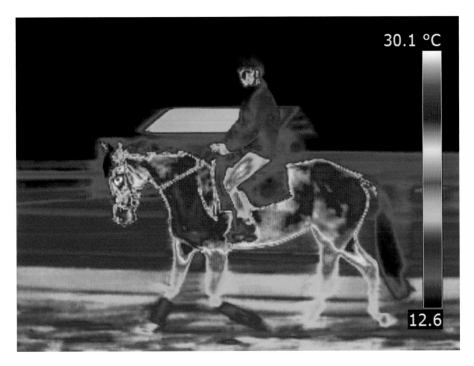

Figure 5.6 The same horse ridden correctly. Note how all the muscles in the dorsal and ventral chains are working, and particularly note the difference of the angle of the pelvis to the previous image, demonstrating the 'bow and string' theory.

These thermal images give a graphic demonstration of the importance of correct schooling, and establishment of balanced dorsal and ventral chains. Only then can correct posture be achieved leading to increased athletic ability and minimum risk of injury.

How do these completely different ways of schooling and working the horse reflect in the appearance of the horse? Photo 5.7 shows a horse that demonstrates good athletic conformation with a strong, well-muscled neck, back and quarters, and toned abdominal muscles, allowing the horse a generous action. The dorsal and ventral chains are working in complete harmony, with the topline long and supple whilst the underline is short and supporting the weight of the horse.

In Photo 5.8, however, you can see a horse at the other end of the spectrum; this animal

Photo 5.7 This horse shows good muscle development, dynamic conformation and athletic movement. (Courtesy of Sam Pawley photography)

has, for whatever reason, a complete breakdown of dorsal and ventral muscular chains and is moving only on the forehand. The almost complete lack of muscle on the back and through the quarters is in strong contradiction to the overdeveloped muscles around the shoulder, base of neck and pectoral area which is entirely indicative of a horse which is unable to utilise the bow and string. The tension in the muscles in the base of the neck in front

Photo 5.8 *above*
A horse that moves predominantly from the forehand, with muscles in the shoulder region and at the base of the neck overdeveloped and sore.

Photo 5.9 Impinging dorsal spinous processes, a condition known as 'kissing spines'. The spinous processes have rubbed against each other causing new bone formation and degenerative disease. (Courtesy of Equine Articulated Skeletons Inc.)

of the scapula is a clear indication that this horse is in pain. This muscle imbalance is completely explained by the previous thermal images.

In addition, notice the dip in front of the withers; this is the classic sign of a horse that is blocking through the shoulder. Effectively the shoulder does not move as it should do as explained in the previous chapter. It is locked in a forward position by the cervical portion of the trapezius muscle, which is why there is muscle spasm at the base of the neck. This occurs at the extreme end of muscular chain breakdown. It is also evident that the horse is developing a sway-backed appearance as the abdominals have lost tone and are no longer able to support the back or abdominal contents. This can predispose the horse to the condition known colloquially as 'kissing spines' when the dorsal spinous processes of the thoracic or lumbar vertebrae impinge upon each other (Photo 5.9). Whilst we now know that many horses may have this condition without showing any symptoms, it can cause quite considerable pain requiring surgery or euthanasia.

The horse in Photo 5.8 has, however, reached the bottom of a very long downward spiral, and it is necessary to be able to recognise a horse that is starting to go wrong, long before he gets to that place.

In Photo 5.10 you see a horse that is on his way down that long spiral. The long muscles along the dorsal line are beginning to waste and become tight, shortening the topline, whilst the ventral line starts to sag and become long. The shoulder and pectoral muscles (which support the forehand) are becoming overdeveloped and sore because the horse is throwing his weight forwards as the 'bow and string' begins to fail and he cannot work properly from behind. This is what we generally term as 'engine at the wrong end' because the horse's poor posture and discomfort have caused him to drag himself along from the front, rather than driving forwards from behind.

As the back becomes increasingly sore a horse seeks ways in which to relieve the pain. Photo 5.11 shows a fit event horse that has qualified for Badminton, but who has become lame because of back and neck pain. You can see that that despite performing at a high level, he shows all the same

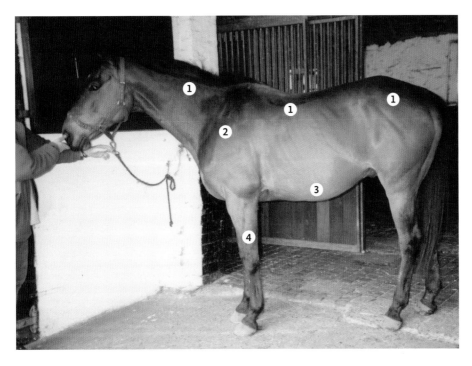

Photo 5.10 Horse showing poor muscle development and posture as a result of incorrect riding.

1 Weak, undermuscled neck, back and gluteal muscles.

2 Overdeveloped shoulder and base of neck muscles.

3 Long, sagging under-line with no abdominal muscle tone.

4 Note how the front legs are camped under as this horse leans heavily on his forehand.

characteristics of the 'engine at the wrong end' syndrome. The shoulder muscles are overdeveloped and the dorsal line is weak.

However, this horse has found a way to help relieve the pain in his back by sitting on his hay net. Horses in this situation will find anything in the stable to sit on, some sit on the door, some on the manger or a window sill. Signs of this behaviour can usually be noticed in the stable as these horses very often do not move from their 'seat' to defecate, and signs of faeces can be seen on sills, mangers or stable walls. If the behaviour has been chronic (of long standing) then you can even see indentations in the semitendinosus muscles that coincide with the height of the sill or manger they are sitting on.

These horses will require veterinary investigation followed by a long course of physiotherapy and remedial schooling (see Chapter 8) to bring them back into correct posture and a pain-free, functioning state.

The causes that start the horse on this journey of muscular-chains breakdown are manifold. It can be an injury, a fall, being cast, poor conformation or poor riding; however, it is much better to be able to recognise the signs in the early stages and seek professional advice before the horse's poor posture and development lead to pain and lameness.

Photo 5.11 The horse with back pain will often find something in the stable to sit on (in this case the hay net) to relieve the pain.

Imaging and treatment of problems

We can see the effects of tight, sore muscles in the back of a horse using thermal imaging.

The thermal image in Figure 5.12 shows a normal horse's back with the dorsal and ventral muscular chains functioning correctly. A symmetry of muscle thermal patterns either side of the vertebral column can be distinguished with no areas of abnormal heat patterns (which would show in bright red) indicative of spasm and pain. Compare this image to Figure 5.13, which is of a horse that demonstrates back pain. Note the bright red colours along the spine under the saddle area.

This horse was diagnosed with pain in the multifidus muscle manifesting when ridden, which was subsequently resolved by a course of physiotherapy and remedial schooling. This was a chronic condition which also

Figure 5.12 Normal thermal image of a horse's back (looking from behind the horse). Note that there is a line of red heat signature (indicative of an inflammatory process) down the vertebral column but the muscles on either side show no signs of abnormal heat and are symmetrical in thermal signature.

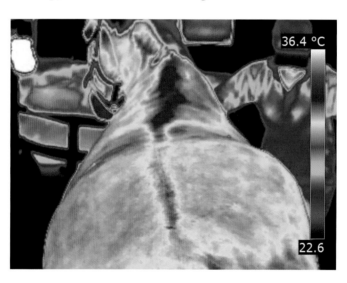

Fig. 5.13 A thermal image of a horse displaying pain on being ridden. Note the bright red colours indicative of heat and pain along the back. The diagnosis was one of multifidus muscle pain.

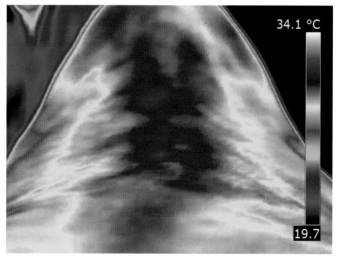

included breakdown of dorsal and ventral muscular chains. Accordingly we can understand how the horse develops pain and tightening of the back in these circumstances.

At this stage it is appropriate to demonstrate how, if an injury is addressed immediately, it can be dealt with and treated very successfully, thus preventing the long downward spiral of posture compensation and muscular chain inhibition, leading to a chronic condition that will cause suffering for the horse plus the financial and emotional costs for the owner of veterinary/physiotherapy treatment.

In Figure 5.14 is a thermal image (from behind) of a horse whose left hind limb had slipped underneath him whilst competing two days previously and sustained a rotational fall. Although the horse was not lame, and the vet had ruled out major injury, the next day the horse presented with the inability to maintain right-lead canter and was becoming disunited behind. The owner was advised by her own vet that the horse had some acute muscle soreness through the back and left gluteal, and should be checked over by a physiotherapist as soon as possible.

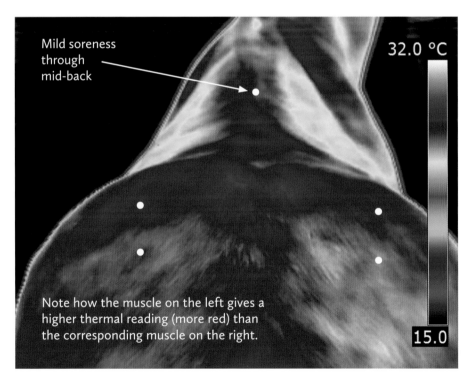

Mild soreness through mid-back

32.0 °C

15.0

Note how the muscle on the left gives a higher thermal reading (more red) than the corresponding muscle on the right.

Figure 5.14 Thermal image of a horse that has sustained a fall whilst competing.

On examination by the physiotherapist the next day (less than 48 hours post-injury), the horse was found to have mild soreness through the back but moderate spasm and pain in the left middle gluteal muscle, which was creating a pelvic rotation.

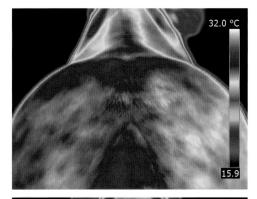

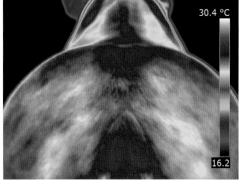

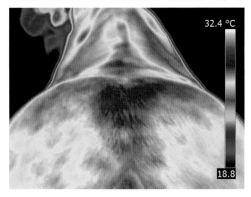

Figure 5.15 *top*
Thirty minutes post-treatment the muscles are relaxing and rehydrating.

Figure 5.16 *centre*
Seventy-five minutes post-treatment the muscles continue to relax and rehydrate.

Fig. 5.17 *bottom*
Now, 120 minutes post-treatment, the muscles are almost fully recovered.

Soft tissue manipulation and mobilisation was applied by the veterinary physiotherapist, and imaging repeated after 30 minutes, 75 minutes and 120 minutes post-treatment. Within 30 minutes post-treatment we can see that the muscles are beginning to relax and rehydrate, thus becoming cooler as the inflammatory mediators are reduced (Figure 5.15). At 75 minutes post-treatment the muscles have continued to release and rehydrate and the thermal patterns on the left and right are nearly symmetrical (Figure 5.16). At 120 minutes post-treatment the horse's muscles are now almost fully recovered (Figure 5.17). All these images were confirmed by palpation of the muscles by the treating physiotherapist.

The reason why this slow release takes place is because the muscles and the fasciae need to rehydrate and the inflammatory mediators need to be removed from the fibres. It is notable that after this type of treatment, the horse needs to rest and drink large amounts of water to enable complete resolution of the muscle spasm and rehydration. When a muscle is in spasm, not only do the fibres shorten, but the fascia contracts and the intercellular fluid is squeezed out. Therefore the fluid needs to be replaced to fully allow the fibres to lengthen and the fascia to expand to allow the rehydration process. It has been demonstrated that it can take up to four hours post-muscle release for the fascia to fully rehydrate, and the muscle to begin to return to full athletic function.[1]

Your physiotherapist will normally recommend 24 hours of rest and turnout before returning to ridden work to allow the body to flush the inflammatory mediators from the muscle into the lymphatic system.

Therefore the take-home message from this is that if you address muscle injury as soon as possible post-trauma, then it can be resolved and prevented from becoming a chronic condition leading to dysfunction of muscular chains and poor posture resulting in pain and loss of athletic function. Indeed at a subsequent physiotherapy assessment the horse in Figure 5.14 had fully recovered and was back to pre-injury performance levels.

1 Schleip et al 2012, *Journal of Bodywork and Movement Therapies*, 16 94–100

As previously discussed, horses have an extraordinary ability to disguise injury by using compensatory gait patterns until such time as they cannot compensate any longer and their athletic performance deteriorates or they become lame. Figure 5.18 is an image of a young warmblood horse that is being trained for eventing and this thermal image was taken whilst the horse was jumping a fence at home. The owner had noticed that the horse worked considerably better on the flat on the left rein (with an inability to sustain right-lead canter) but jumped considerably better off the right rein. The horse is not clinically lame and the vet had referred the horse for physiotherapy.

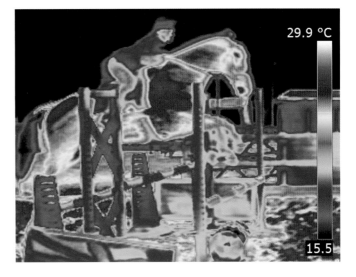

Figure 5.18 Thermal image of a horse jumping. Note the warm thermal patterns over the shoulders and the middle gluteal.

In the thermal image you can see that the muscles of the shoulder are working particularly hard, as is the middle gluteal in the hindquarters.

Photo 5.19 is a photograph of the horse in Figure 5.18, jumping the same fence at the same time as the thermal image was taken. In fact, you can see the thermographer, Helen Morrell of Surrey Vet Physio, taking the thermal image on the right of the picture. However, of note in the photograph is the placement of the hind feet. It can be seen that the horse is greatly favouring the right hind limb to jump off. Compare this hind limb posture to that seen in an elite jumping horse in Photo 5.20 where

Photo 5.19 Photograph of the warmblood in the previous figure; this photo was taken at the same time as the thermal image. Note the asymmetrical placement of the hind feet.

Photo 5.20 An elite jumping horse with good athletic posture uses both hind limbs equally in the take-off phase. (Courtesy of Nico Morgan)

take-off has utilised both hind limbs symmetrically and the hind feet are still together in flight.

In jumping disciplines, synchrony of the hind limbs at the take-off phase is vital. We discussed in Chapter 4 how the forces of the hind limb act against the rigid strut of the lumbar vertebrae to propel the horse forwards and upwards. If one hind limb is weaker than the other, or they are not used synchronously, the athletic jumping ability is seriously impaired. In fact, if you review the illustration of the 'jumping skeleton' in Chapter 4, it can be seen how important hind limb synchrony in take-off is.

When a thermal image is taken of the young horse in Figure 5.18 and Photo 5.19 post-jumping exercise, the results of this compensatory gait pattern are clear to see (Figure 5.21). The large locomotor muscles in the right hind are considerably warmer than those in the left, which barely show any response to exercise at all. Therefore the horse has been protecting the left hind, resulting in the ridden differences reported by the rider. As there was no presenting injury or lameness this gait pattern has arisen as a result of chronic locomotor compensation which may have originally been caused by injury which was not fully addressed at the time.

This completely explains the problems that the horse was displaying in that the right-rein canter could not be sustained because of the weak left hind, but he could jump off the right hind.

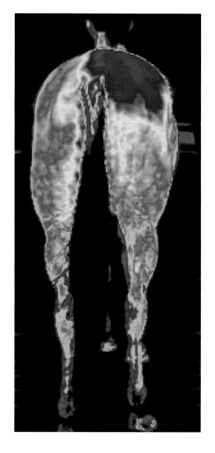

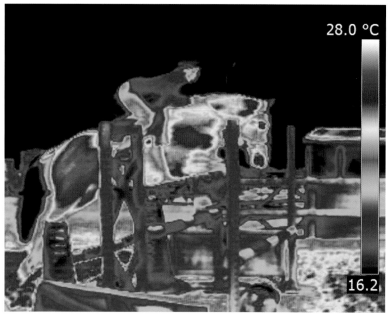

Figure 5.21 *left* Note the asymmetrical thermal patterns with the right-hind locomotor muscles having a much warmer signature than the left.

Figure 5.22 *above* An elite jumping pony jumping the same fence as the horse in Figure 5.18. This pony makes far more use of the hindquarters and less use of his shoulder (as should be the case).

The ability of the owner of this horse to pick up on small issues arising during the course of normal training such as the horse showing different capabilities on different reins is, therefore, very important. There is no doubt that the postural compensations being displayed by the horse, whilst not yet causing lameness, would in all probability in a short period of time have gone on to have so overloaded that right hind limb that lameness was bound to occur.

Indeed if we consider the thermal image of an elite jumping pony (Figure 5.22) being ridden by the same rider, over the same fence and on the same day as the horse in Figure 5.18, there are many differences in the thermal patterns displayed by both animals.

The pony uses the hindquarters considerably more, and the shoulder considerably less, than the young horse with the postural problems. Because the young horse cannot use the hindquarters effectively, he places a heavy reliance on the forehand.

But all is not lost for the young horse. After treatment by Gail we can see him in Photo 5.23 jumping cross-country using both hind limbs equally, and starting to win competitions. Because his posture has been corrected, he can become the sport horse that his owner deserves, and is not started

Photo 5.23 The young horse now jumps using both hind limbs after physiotherapy treatment.

on the downward spiral of postural compensations that would lead inevitably to injury.

So now we begin to get an appreciation of the importance of posture in the horse whatever function we put him to. Well-developed posture leads to strong dorsal and ventral muscular chains, effective bow and string function, maximum lumbosacral-joint movement, balance, athletic prowess and minimum risk of injury.

Right at the beginning of this book we emphasised that posture is the key to having the horse of your dreams, whether you want a happy hacker/trail horse or the elite athlete. In this chapter we have demonstrated this using thermal imaging. In the next chapters we will look at many of the problems you will encounter on your way to this goal, and how you can overcome them.

CHAPTER SIX

Saddles, Riders and Girths:

How they affect the horse

Domesticity and the use of the horse

We have domesticated the horse over thousands of years. When an animal is domesticated it effectively means that evolution has produced a partnership. In the case of horses and humans we each had much to offer the other and the partnership was beneficial to both: humans protected the horse from predators and provided them with food, and the horse became a beast of burden for humans, carrying us and other items that needed to be transported.

To a large extent, the horse that exists today is far removed from the one with which our ancestors were involved. This divide is made all the more obvious by the fact that we in First World countries developed the concept of the 'sport horse'. Whilst horses have been used for centuries for racing and hunting, these activities were solely the domain of the landed gentry who could afford the cost and keep of several horses and had the income and time to indulge in leisure activity.

In current times, horses have become a leisure activity for many more people, and the concept of DIY livery means that the costs of owning a horse are within the realms of an even greater number of people who also have more leisure time. It is now thought that as many as one in five households in the UK has a connection with horses. A number of services have built up to support this booming ownership of horses, some good and some not so good.

There are, however, two things that must be applied to the horse for us to ride: tack and the rider, and both can cause a significant amount of damage to the horse. Although allowances can be made for riders of differing skills, there is no excuse for poorly fitting tack.

Saddle fitting

Gail has calculated that about 85 per cent of horses that are referred to her for back pain or remedial schooling have some form of chronic saddle damage. Nothing can cause so much harm to your horse as a poorly fitting saddle, and Gail has spent a good deal of time trying to understand how to get the best saddle fit for her clients. However, she has come to the conclusion that even the best-fitting saddle can cause some restriction of movement, and it is simply the degree of that restriction that is important.

As we demonstrated in Chapter 4, the saddle sits over the thoracic vertebrae just behind the shoulder region. In that chapter we stressed the vital importance of shoulder movement. The shoulder blade (scapula) needs to glide forwards and backwards over the ribs associated with the shoulder region and any restriction of this movement will result in a shortened stride in the front limb, and interrupt the functioning of the dorsal muscular chain. Yet where do we place the saddle? The answer is just behind the shoulder, and far too many riders place the saddle too far forwards, completely restricting the backwards movement of the scapula. Take another look at the equine skeleton in this region (Photo 6.1)

As the shoulder slides backwards and forwards over the thoracic vertebrae in the shoulder region, a soft-tissue structure arises from the ventral (top) region which is able to change shape to accommodate the contours of the dorsal spinous processes. This is known as the scapular cartilage. A number of muscles originate from the scapular cartilage including the infraspinatus, supraspinatus and the subscapularis.

The raised ridge down the middle of the scapula is called the scapular spine, and muscles that move the shoulder backwards and forwards insert on the scapular spine. Predominantly it is the trapezius muscle (see Chapters 2 and 4) which has a cervical (neck) portion and a thoracic portion, each of which can contract independently of the other (Figure 6.2).

If the cervical portion contracts it lifts and pulls the scapula forwards, but if the thoracic portion contracts it pulls the scapula backwards. Each portion of the trapezius muscle should have about equal strength and mass,

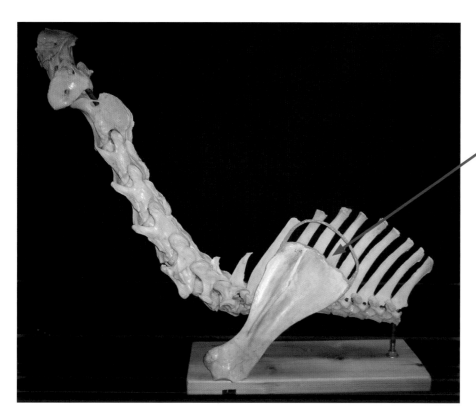

Photo 6.1 The equine shoulder blade showing location of scapular cartilage (Courtesy of Equine Articulated Skeletons Inc.)

This area is occupied by the scapular cartilage, a soft tissue structure that can change shape to accommodate the backwards and forwards movement of the shoulder blade.

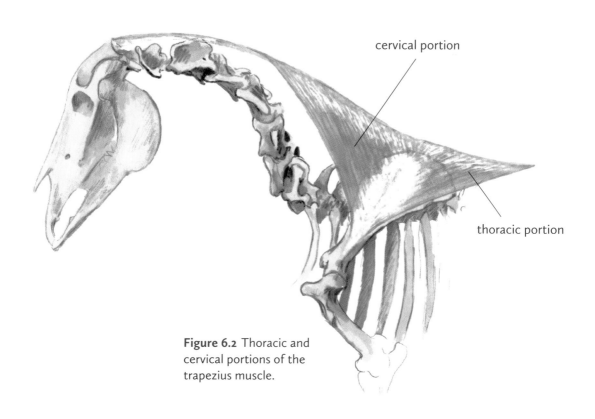

cervical portion

thoracic portion

Figure 6.2 Thoracic and cervical portions of the trapezius muscle.

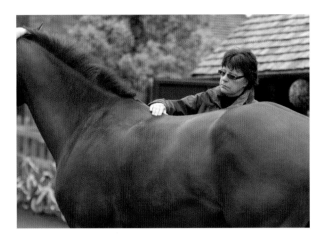

Photo 6.3 In the functioning horse, with no saddle damage, the thoracic and cervical portions of the trapezius should be balanced, with neither portion having dominance.

as is demonstrated on surface anatomy by the horse in Photo 6.3, where Gail's hand is resting on the thoracic portion of the trapezius.

However, let's have another look at the horse with chronic damage to the ventral muscular chain (Photo 6.4) but this time concentrate on the shoulder area.

It is clear that the cervical portion of the trapezius is dominant because the thoracic part has completely wasted. But why has this happened; is it poor schooling or bad saddle fit? We demonstrated in the previous chapter that badly schooled horses over-use the muscles at the base of the neck like the cervical trapezius, but it could equally be poor saddle fit. In fact, the answer is that they have both probably contributed to the current parlous state of this horse.

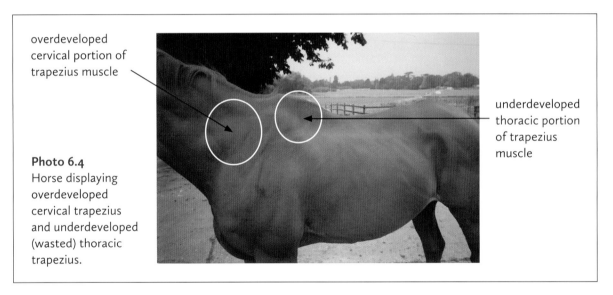

overdeveloped cervical portion of trapezius muscle

underdeveloped thoracic portion of trapezius muscle

Photo 6.4 Horse displaying overdeveloped cervical trapezius and underdeveloped (wasted) thoracic trapezius.

Let us consider the saddle aspect, because that is probably the main culprit, especially in the later stages. The first question to ask is 'How do I know if my saddle fits?' In Gail's experience there are several answers that people give and the following are some of the most common ones.

- I had it specially made for him (usually several years before!)

- The saddle fitter came out when I bought him (again usually a long time ago) and told me this one fitted.

- The saddle came with the horse when I bought him.

- I find it very comfortable for me.

- It fitted my last horse.

- I use a sheepskin pad and a gel pad together (or substitute any other kinds of multiple pad combinations) underneath just in case.

- It was the only one I could afford.

Very rarely is the correct answer given which would be: 'I did a lot of research into finding the right saddle for my horse and me, and I found a saddle maker/fitter who was highly recommended and I ask him/her to come back every six months to check the fit. I also ask my physiotherapist to check for signs of saddle damage in my horse every six months.'

It is not in the remit of this book to go into the ins and outs of saddle fit, and it is something that you need to read about elsewhere, but there is now an increasing body of evidence in the literature about the vital importance of correct saddle fit and how poor saddle fit can affect your horse. However, the generalised history of dorsal muscular chain damage caused by poor saddle fit is as follows, particularly for those of us who grew up in the Pony Club who were taught only two things about saddles.

1. Make sure you can get at least three fingers breadth between the withers and the pommel (to make sure it doesn't rub).

2. Make sure you can pull the District Commissioner's whip through from front to back of the saddle whilst it is on the horse (to make sure that the gullet is wide enough).

They are probably the two worst possible bits of advice you can get for saddle fit, but most likely it is the first one that causes the most problems. In Gail's experience the most common scenario is the rider is so paranoid about the pommel coming into contact with the horse that 'just to be safe' they either fit a saddle that is slightly too narrow, or think that putting some sort of thick pad underneath will 'protect' the back. The problem with putting thick pads underneath a saddle is that where the saddle sits either side of the withers (which is where the points of the tree are) this actually compresses the muscle and constricts the blood flow to the area. It is like putting on a thick pair of socks when your shoes are too tight – the effect is the reverse of what you are trying to achieve.

This is effectively the same as fitting a saddle that is too narrow, and where either the thick pad or the too-narrow saddle sits on top of the thoracic trapezius muscle, the blood flow to that muscle is constricted.

Where the blood capillaries are constricted, the muscle fibres that they are supplying with oxygen and other nutrients become starved and wasted. As the muscle wastes, the pommel of the saddle drops. The rider then thinks that the saddle is now too wide and fits another narrower saddle – and the process is repeated until the muscle is completely wasted and the points of the saddle are digging into the back of the shoulder blade, causing pain and restricting the backwards movement of the shoulder.

Of course it is not *just* the trapezius muscle that suffers, it is the deeper muscles as well including the latissimus dorsi, the multifidus and the longissimus dorsi. Therefore what has now happened is that two main areas of functional equine movement and athletic ability, the balance of muscular chains and the scapular glide, fail to function. Because the cervical portion of the trapezius is now dominant over the thoracic part, and because the points of the saddle are digging in behind the shoulder, the scapula becomes locked forwards. This restricts the protraction of the forelimb and to many riders and trainers this looks and feels as if the horse is resisting, and failing to go forwards correctly. It also prevents the folding up of the front limbs when jumping and very often the first indication the rider gets that there is a problem is that the horse starts to take the top bar of the jump off with his front feet.

The dorsal muscular chain fails and the muscles in the topline become wasted, tight and short whilst the ventral chain becomes slack and long with no muscle tone in the abdominals. The ventral line cannot now change the angle of the pelvis and the movement in the lumbosacral junction deteriorates. The hind limb cannot now be placed correctly underneath the body and the hamstrings become tight and short, further increasing the impression that he is refusing to go forwards. But he is not refusing to go forwards correctly; he is simply not physically capable of doing so. Remember that **not physically capable** is one of our three main reasons for horses not doing what we want.

The horse is now forced to move on the forehand and the whole descending vicious spiral goes on, exacerbated by the rider using spurs or a whip because she thinks the horse is resisting or lazy, until the pain is too much and the horse starts to object. At what point the horse objects depends on the predisposing temperament of the horse, some will start to object very soon, but others will continue to try for a long time, disguising their pain, until the pain becomes too much. This may manifest in rearing, spinning, refusing jumps or any other attempt to get rid of the rider. The horse is then labelled 'bad'. So finally we have reached our third main reason for a horse not doing what we want him to do, **pain**, and all because the saddle was too tight.

We can demonstrate this with a case history. Let's take another look at the horse from the previous chapter that has started along this long line of postural change, but not got to the end (Photo 6.5). We have put little white dots on the horse to draw attention to the tell-tale signs.

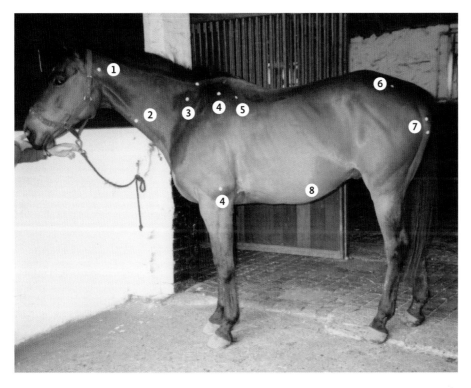

Photo 6.5 The horse demonstrating the early signs of poor posture and breakdown of dorsal and ventral muscular chains.

1 Overdeveloped rectus capitus.

2 Overdeveloped sternocephalicus.

3 Cervical trapezius is dominant and dips in front of withers.

4 Overdeveloped shoulder muscles.

5 Thoracic trapezius wasted.

6 Gluteal muscles underdeveloped.

7 Overdeveloped hamstrings.

8 Sagging abdomen resulting from ventral chain disruption.

- The rectus capitus muscle is overdeveloped because there is a constant fight between the rider's hand and the horse's mouth. The rider is attempting to force the head and neck into an outline, which the horse is not capable of presenting.

- Again, the sternocephalicus muscle is overdeveloped because the horse is going around with his head in the air so that he can drag himself along on the forehand.

- The cervical trapezius is dominant and the shoulder muscles are overdeveloped because the horse is constantly on the forehand, and the scapula is being locked forwards.

- The thoracic trapezius is wasted and ineffective in retracting the scapula.

- Because the dorsal chain is not functioning and the horse is not working through from behind, the 'engine' of the gluteal muscles is not functioning correctly and becomes underdeveloped when compared with the overdeveloped shoulders.

- Because the horse cannot bring his hind limb underneath him correctly the semitendinosis and semimembranosus (hamstring) muscles are shortened and tight.

- Because the dorsal muscular chain cannot lengthen, the ventral chain cannot contract, and all abdominal tone is lost.

Having looked at this horse from the side, let us have a look along his back (Photo 6.6). Studying the horse from this view is always useful because you can see any asymmetry in muscular development. However, a word of warning here; never get behind a horse like this if you are unsure of him. If there is any doubt at all in your mind that he could kick out, you can put the horse in the stable with his quarters towards the door, and you can stand outside the door.

Photo 6.6 Looking down the back of the horse in Photo 6.5.

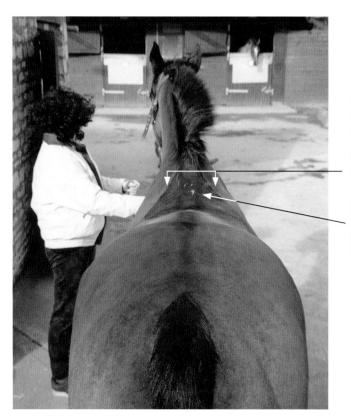

note the lack of muscle behind the shoulders and either side of the withers

patches of white hair denoting previous saddle rubbing/sores

In this photo you can clearly see the lack of muscle in the thoracic trapezius region, and also the telltale white patches of hair indicating this horse has had previous trouble with saddles. However, as we have said, this horse is by no means as far down the spiral as the horse in Photo 6.4, and if the owner or trainer can spot these problems as this stage, then it would not take too much time to get him right.

However, if not identified at this time it can go very badly wrong and if you look at Photo 6.7 you can see the same horse as in Photo 6.6 but only four months later. See how much more muscle has been lost in the thoracic trapezius region, but now the long muscles of the back are wasting as well as can be seen by the spine now being more prominent. Also, and to prove the point about the saddle pommel dropping as the muscle wastes, you can observe two more patches of white hair demonstrating further saddle rubs/sores have occurred during this short period of time.

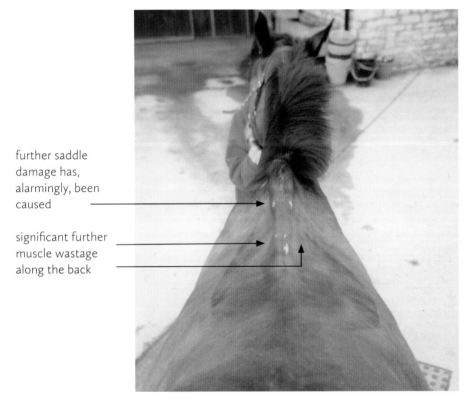

Photo 6.7 The same horse as in Fig. 6.6 just four months later, showing how much more damage has been caused over a short period of time.

further saddle damage has, alarmingly, been caused

significant further muscle wastage along the back

Now we need to look at the saddle that is currently being used on this horse (Photos 6.8 and 6.9) and there is very little good that can be said about it.

The panels are seen to be very asymmetrical with the panel on the right curving in towards the gullet at the cantle. The saddle is old and the gullet is off-centre which will make it sit asymmetrically on the horse. In fact, when it is placed on the saddle rack (Photo 6.9) just how asymmetrically it sits is plain to see, and this is how it sits on the horse. Again, it is not for us to discuss saddle construction and fit, but to show you how good saddle fit and an understanding of the interaction of saddles with equine function is vital for you and your horse. This saddle is not only uncomfortable and ill-fitting for the horse, it is also dangerous for the rider who cannot possibly adopt a secure seat when the saddle sits as this one does.

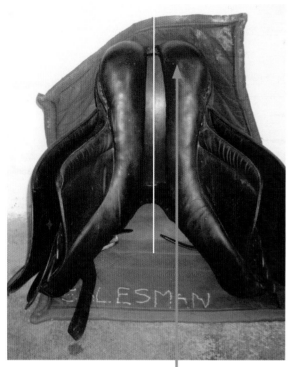 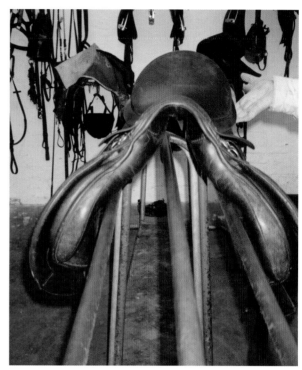

Photo 6.8 *above left* The panels are very unequal with the one on the right curving in towards the centre of the gullet. The white line is a straight line from the centre of the pommel showing that the gullet is off-centre.

Photo 6.9 *above right* Note how asymmetrically the saddle sits.

note how this panel curves inwards towards the centre of the gullet

How saddle fit affects lateral flexion

This is probably a good point at which to introduce the effects of saddles on lateral flexion. In previous chapters, we have shown how there is some limited lateral flexion in the thoracic vertebrae that lie underneath the saddle area. Clearly without a saddle that lateral flexion can be allowed without hindrance. But the very construction of a classic English saddle is for panels that sit securely either side of the vertebral column. That saddle is then 'bedded down' by a girth and, finally, the rider sits on top of it. Therefore all this must interfere with the lateral flexion of the area under the saddle.

This becomes evident if you are able to get a view from above a ridden horse performing a lateral movement such as half-pass. It then is clear that most, if not all, lateral flexion comes from the neck, the function of the thoracic sling and the small amount of lumbosacral flexion. This then makes the function of the shoulder and thoracic sling paramount in more advanced dressage movements.

Even the best-fitting saddle will, therefore, cause restriction of movement in a lateral plane but, as outlined earlier in the chapter, it is the degree of that restriction that is important, and unbalanced saddles such as the one shown opposite will cause a large degree of restriction, not only to lateral flexion but to the action of the thoracic sling, and the dorsal and ventral muscular chains. The only thing you can do to minimise this restriction is to ensure that your saddle is a perfect fit for your horse. In addition, although there is no quantifiable scientific evidence, Gail's experience leads her to believe that saddle panels filled with air, such as the Cair™ system found in Bates and Wintec saddles, allow slightly more freedom in a lateral plane than do flock-filled saddle panels. Another of the benefits of these air-filled panels is that they do not become asymmetrical over time. All but the very top-class riders will favour one hip and will sit fractionally asymmetrically, leading to the panel taking more of the rider's weight and will compress (if flocked filled) over time making the panels asymmetrical, whereas the air-filled panel will not.

Rider Asymmetry

Whilst on the subject of riders sitting asymmetrically, such problems can be observed by using the Visualise™ System created by Russell Guire of Centaur Biomechanics as part of their rider assessment programme. In Figure 6.10 there is a view of a horse and rider from behind, and reflective markers have been placed in strategic points for data capture (there will be a full discussion of the Centaur Biomechanics systems in the next chapter). The Visualise™ jacket worn by the rider has reflective strips running down the rider's spinal column and a strip across the shoulders, so if the rider is sitting correctly there will be a perfectly symmetrical cross formed by these strips.

Reflective markers are placed on the centre of the back of the riding helmet, the centre of the cantle on the saddle, the pelvic symphysis between the tuber sacrale and on the top of the tail. A correctly positioned rider and saddle should show a perfectly straight, perpendicular line through all those markers, which clearly in this case, is not happening.

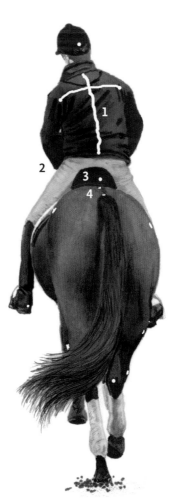

Figure 6.10 The Visualise™ system demonstrating the saddle is slipping to the right (photo from which this original drawing was drawn courtesy of Russell Guire, Centaur Biomechanics)

1 This line should be perpendicular but the rider is leaning to the left, which accounts for the saddle slipping to the right.

2 The rider is collapsing through the left hip.

3 The marker on the centre of the cantle clearly showing saddle is sitting to the right.

4 The marker on the cantle should be in line with this marker on the horse's spine.

You can see that the rider's weight is not equal on both sides of the saddle, thus making both the horse and rider unbalanced. Such a posture would have been evident in the horse seen in Photo 6.7 wearing the saddle seen in Photo 6.9.

How this problem arises needs careful investigation from both a qualified saddle fitter and a veterinary physiotherapist, as in all likelihood the saddle is slipping because of an asymmetric saddle and an asymmetric rider, and not only will the saddle need to be rectified but the horse and rider will also need therapy.

The effects of such a situation can be ameliorated, however, if the saddle has Cair™ panels incorporating the Bates Easy Change System™. Not only can these prevent asymmetrical panels developing, they can give support to the asymmetrical rider, and they are Gail's saddle of choice for correcting horse and rider asymmetry.

Look at Photos 6.11a and b; they are a prime example of horse and rider asymmetry. This lady had sustained a fractured pelvis some years before which made her sit to the left. Over the months of her riding this horse, this imbalance has created asymmetrical muscle development in the horse and if you look carefully you can see that the muscle over the horse's quarters on the left drops away when compared with that on the right. This is obvious in Photo 6.11a when the horse is not supporting saddle or rider but all the more obvious in Photo 6.11b when saddle and rider are in place. This asymmetry continued through the long muscles of the back with those on the left wasting. The rider thinks she is sitting square with her stirrups equal but, because of her previous injury, the right stirrup is much shorter than the left. Again a vicious cycle is created with the rider sitting to the left, leading to the left muscles on the horse's back wasting, leading to the saddle and rider slipping more to the left, leading to more muscle wastage … And so it goes on.

Gail used a new Bates/Wintec saddle to correct this lady's riding posture and allow her horse to be more balanced. To do that, use of the Bates Easy Change™ system enabled Gail to lift the left hand side of the saddle until the rider was sitting correctly (Photo 6.12). Adjustment of the Bates' saddles is simple, takes only minutes and needs no special tools, and Gail can usually adapt them to compensate for any horse/rider problems.

Although initially the rider will not feel balanced, careful instruction over the next few weeks will allow the owner to ride her horse, whilst Gail corrects the muscle imbalance in the horse. As the horse becomes more symmetrical Gail can adjust the saddle to accommodate that.

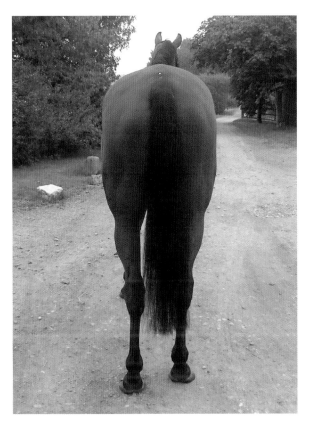

Photos 6.11a and b Asymmetrical horse and rider. a) *above* The horse without saddle or rider shows asymmetry in the quarters. b) *above right* Both the saddle and rider are slipping to the left and the rider's right stirrup is three holes shorter than the left stirrup.

Photo 6.12 The left hand side of the saddle has been lifted using the Bates Easy Change System™ correcting the rider's posture and taking into account the muscle asymmetry in the horse. The saddle and the rider are now sitting centrally.

To appreciate the differences in the interaction between the saddle panels of the owner's old saddle and the horse's back compared with the interaction of the panels in the new Bates saddle and the horse's back, we can use thermography to look at the thermal profiles of each saddle after the horse and rider have completed a standardised exercise test.

In Figure 6.13 we can see the owner's old saddle. The thermal patterns on each panel are completely different with the red areas indicating friction between the panel and the horse's back. If you think about how this saddle was sitting off to the left, with the back of the right panel sitting over the spine and the rider's weight thrown to the back of the left panel, you can appreciate how the right panel was rubbing on the spine whilst the greater friction profile seen at the back of the left panel indicates where most of the rider's weight was located.

If you look at the wither area at the front of the panels, the right panel shows a greater thermal pattern because the rider was causing the saddle to compress against the right side of the withers as the saddle slipped to the left. Accordingly this saddle was creating a number of friction areas, and the horse's back was reflecting this abnormal thermal pattern.

When the horse and rider undergo the standard exercise test in the new Bates Saddle after fitting by Gail, and the Cair™ panels are thermally imaged, you can see a completely different thermal profile (Figure 6.14) to that of the owner's old saddle.

Figure 6.13 *below* Thermal imaging of the owner's old saddle after riding a standard exercise test: note the greater friction profile at the back of the left panel when compared to the right; there is also a greater friction profile over the right wither area.

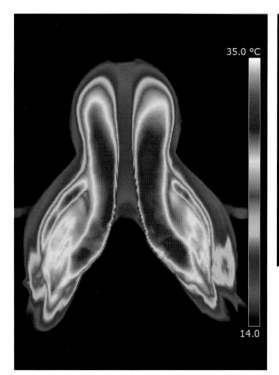

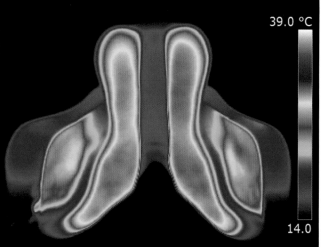

Figure 6.14 *above* The newly fitted Bates saddle with Cair™ air panels thermally imaged after the horse and rider have completed the standardised exercise test. Note the completely different thermal profile to that of the old saddle in Figure 6.13.

Firstly, if you compare the construction of both saddles you will immediately appreciate that the Bates saddle has a wider gullet and the panels are wider and flatter, providing a greater surface area over the back. For the avoidance of doubt, this is not confined to the Bates saddle, but accords with best practice in ensuring that the rider's weight is distributed over a greater area, decreasing possible friction or bridging problems.

However, the Bates saddle has allowed simple adjustment to compensate for the rider's poor posture, and for the resultant muscle loss on the left back muscles. The weight of the rider is now almost perfectly symmetrical, and causing no areas of friction. In fact, there is a fractionally higher thermal profile on the right panel of the new saddle, most probably caused by the rider over-compensating for her new position in the saddle. The physical problems of the horse and rider can now be addressed by the physiotherapist.

With this horse we had a combination of rider and saddle causing problems, which problem caused the other is a 'chicken and egg' question, and practically it does not matter which came first. The important take-home message is that the rider/saddle/horse interface needs to be regularly monitored by a qualified saddle fitter and a veterinary physiotherapist.

Once these problems were addressed, the horse became considerably freer in movement and obviously much more comfortable. The previous saddle and the rider's posture had created pain which resulted in the horse becoming lethargic and unwilling to work.

Another problem that Gail encounters is when a rider has a wide horse but is using a saddle that is far too narrow simply because the rider cannot physically accommodate a wide saddle that would fit the horse. This situation creates a real paradox – the narrow saddle damages the horse, but a wider saddle would damage the rider!

Very recently a new Swedish saddle design has become available which may resolve this problem. This is the Rebel™ Saddle which is constructed in two parts. The first part, including the saddle panels is intended to fit the horse, whilst the second part being the seat is intended to fit the rider. In this way both the horse and the rider can be comfortable. The seat can be designed for jumping, dressage etc. (Photos 6.15a–c, see overleaf)

There is precious little literature in the scientific field about the effects of saddles and riders on movement but the general impression to be gained from those that do exist is that the flexion of the lumbar vertebrae are restricted (affecting lumbosacral movement) and that the saddle and rider represents a significant influence in back movements. We know that there

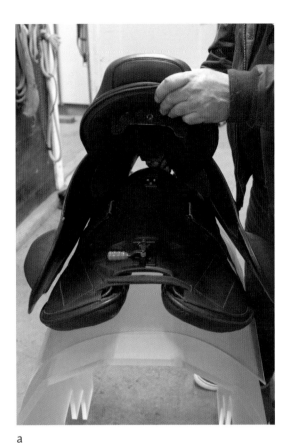

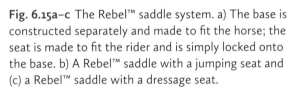

a

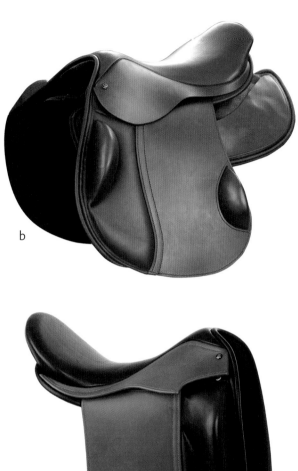

b

Fig. 6.15a–c The Rebel™ saddle system. a) The base is constructed separately and made to fit the horse; the seat is made to fit the rider and is simply locked onto the base. b) A Rebel™ saddle with a jumping seat and (c) a Rebel™ saddle with a dressage seat.

c

is an inextricable link between limb movements and excursions of the back due to the dorsal muscular chain, particularly the longissimus dorsi which is one of the most powerful muscles influencing back movement, and also the middle gluteal muscle which is instrumental for propulsion.[2] We also know that retraction of the forelimb and protraction of the hind limb both flex the back. Therefore even the best-fitting saddles and skilled riders have a deleterious effect upon the movement of the horse, but the worse either get, the more the detrimental effect on locomotion.

2 P. de Coco, P.R van Weeren and W. Back. 'Effects of girth, saddle and weight on movements of the horse' *Equine Veterinary Journal* (2004) 36 (8) 758–763

Please do not underestimate the deleterious effects of badly constructed/fitted saddles. Whilst it is appreciated that saddles are not cheap pieces of equipment to buy, their fit is paramount for the comfort and movement of your horse. However, do not mistake 'expensive' for 'good fit'. We have seen some very expensive saddles which fit the horse very badly, and some very inexpensive saddles that fit very well such as the Wintec with Cair™ panels. If your horse is more comfortable he will be more willing to work forwards than if he is in pain. When you consider how poorly fitting saddles affect the way a horse moves, ensuring that your horse has the best saddle fit could mean the difference between winning and coming tenth. Surely that thought alone should spur you into checking your saddle fit.

Girths

Even if you have a well-fitting saddle, very often no-one gives any consideration to the girth. After all the girth is just a tool for securing the saddle isn't it? Well actually no it isn't and girths can cause damage to your horse and impede his movement and athletic potential.

Gail's top tips for girth fitting are as follows.

1. If you have elastic on one side of the girth, the final tightening of the girth should be done from the non-elasticated end. If it is done from the elasticated end, especially whilst the rider is in the saddle, it can pull the saddle over to that side, causing long-term problems.

2. For the reasons above, do not use a girth with elastic on both ends.

3. If you have long straps on your dressage saddle, make sure that your girth is long enough that the buckles do not sit behind the elbows. If the buckles are sitting behind the elbow then as the horse moves, as the elbow moves backwards, it will hit the buckle causing discomfort and thereby shortening the stride.

4. Do not over-tighten the girth. By doing this you will impede the horse's breathing, and constrict the muscles beneath the girth causing restriction of movement.

There is one very recent piece of research that demonstrates how much girths can affect your horse's movement. This research looks at the effects of one particular, newly designed girth, the Fairfax Girth, developed by Vanessa Fairfax of Fairfax Saddles (Photos 6.16a and b).

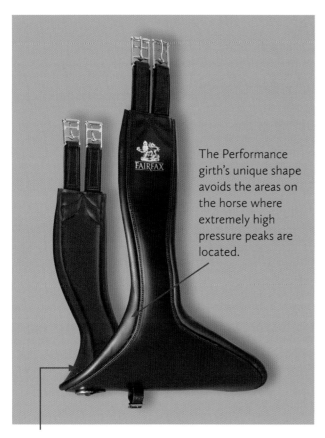

The Performance girth's unique shape avoids the areas on the horse where extremely high pressure peaks are located.

A Prolite cushioned buffer zone guides the muscle bulk under the girth rather than blocking it.

Photos 6.16a and b The Fairfax girth helps to increase freedom of movement and thus improves performance. a) *left* The Fairfax girth's unique shape and cushioned zone. b) *below* This photo shows how the standard gauge girth sits on the horse, avoiding high pressure areas.

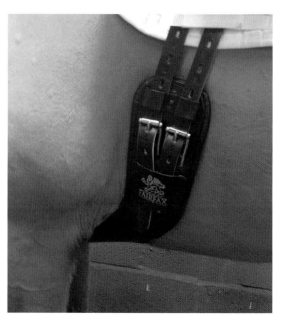

Being a rider and competitor herself, Vanessa was very much aware of the problems that girths could cause, and decided to develop one that would allow the horse the greatest freedom of movement. Having decided on a design that she thought would work she took an unusual step in the tack manufacturers' sector in deciding to prove, using scientific, quantitative methods that the Fairfax Girth was capable of increasing equine performance. Teaming up with the Animal Health Trust, Centaur Biomechanics, Pliance Saddle Pressure Measuring and the British Equestrian Federation World Class Programme, a fully objective series of tests were conducted with the girth.

Firstly, using the telemetric Pliance pressure measuring system in which pressure sensors were placed between the girth and the horse during locomotion (Photo 6.17), the Fairfax girth was shown to reduce peak pressure profiles by up to 82 per cent when compared to testing of the horse's own girth. Figure 6.18 is a graph of the average pressure profiles of an Olympic dressage horse's own girth when compared to being ridden in the Fairfax Girth in various gaits.

Photo 6.17 *above* The Pliance pressure system monitors the feedback from sensors placed between the girth and the horse. On the left hand side of the computer screen can be seen the pressure profiles from the girth in real time as the horse moves.

Figure 6.18 *below* Pressure testing average results comparing an Olympic dressage horse's own girth to that of the Fairfax in variants of the trot gait.

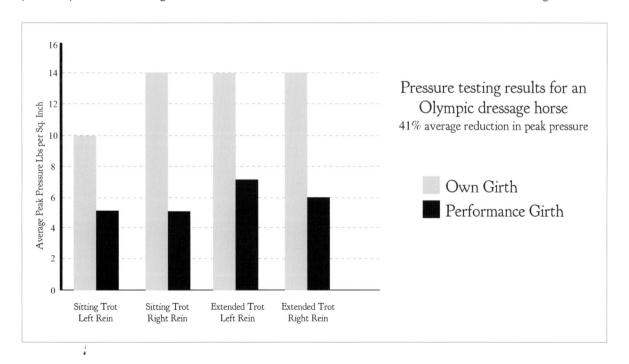

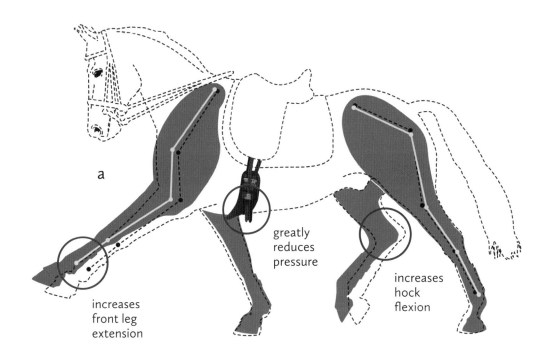

a

greatly
reduces
pressure

increases
hock
flexion

increases
front leg
extension

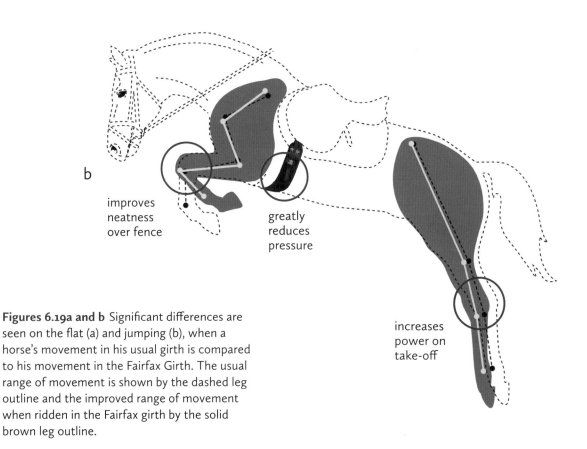

b

improves
neatness
over fence

greatly
reduces
pressure

increases
power on
take-off

Figures 6.19a and b Significant differences are
seen on the flat (a) and jumping (b), when a
horse's movement in his usual girth is compared
to his movement in the Fairfax Girth. The usual
range of movement is shown by the dashed leg
outline and the improved range of movement
when ridden in the Fairfax girth by the solid
brown leg outline.

Having demonstrated that there was a significant reduction of girth pressure from the Fairfax, the next test was to assess whether there was any appreciable effect on movement. Computerised gait analysis was carried out by Centaur Biomechanics (see Chapter 7) to capture differences in horses' movement between using their own girth and the Fairfax girth, both in flat work and in jumping. Their findings are encapsulated in Figures 6.19a and b (see opposite page).

As a consequence of these findings, the British Equestrian Federation requested that the results should not be published until after the London Olympic Games in 2012, where the Fairfax Girth was acclaimed as contributing to the British Team's success, and our 'secret weapon'.

Hopefully we can start to make quantitative analyses of many other items of tack in this manner, so that we can know what designs of tack can help us to keep our horses sound and moving at their optimum.

CHAPTER SEVEN

Gait Analysis and Foot Balance

'HANDSOME IS AS HANDSOME DOES' is a saying we all know. However, we are constantly reminded that good conformation is the key to good movement. What good conformation *is* exactly is hotly debated and, to a large extent, athletic conformation depends on the sporting discipline at which the horse is aimed.

For example, the long back of the Cleveland Bay horse would be considered to be a conformation weakness in a riding horse, but for a carriage horse (which is what the Cleveland Bay was bred for) it is a sought after trait because it improves the ability to pull weights and makes the horse less likely to sustain overreach injuries.

A straight hind leg is also frowned upon, but we know that a straight hind limb enables a greater stride frequency, so it is a benefit in the speed horse. So perhaps 'Handsome is as handsome does' is a good principle to bear in mind, and we should not discard a horse because he does not conform to some erratically researched rules. There are myriad books available dealing with conformation in detail; detail we will not go into here as this book relates only to function.

Athletic ability and good function in the horse is governed by the principle of levers. In moving animals, levers govern the movements of joints and the more efficient the levers, the more efficient the movement; and the principles of 'conformation' were derived from an ideal vision of equine levers. A lever is a rigid structure, fixed at a single point, to which two forces are applied at two different points. One force is 'resistance' and the other is 'effort'. The fixed point is known as the 'fulcrum'. There are three classes of levers, and the one that dominates movement of equine joints is a third-class lever where the resistance and the fulcrum are on opposite sides of the effort, colloquially known as the 'wheelbarrow'.

This lever system provides two important functions. Firstly it increases the effect of an applied force in much the same way as lifting the handles of a laden wheelbarrow makes moving the contents easier. The second function is to increase the speed or velocity of joint movement. Imagine you are picking up a mug of coffee. The weight of the mug is the resistance; the effort to pick it up is applied by your biceps muscle, and the fulcrum is the centre of rotation of your elbow joint. To follow this line would take us into the highly complex mathematical science of biomechanics, but this is also not the aim of this book. We hope to be able to deliver 'applied' biomechanics in such a way for you to appreciate the function of the horse, and use that knowledge to improve your horse's movement, posture and athleticism.

Gait analysis

In Chapters 2, 3 and 4 we listed the major muscles of movement and their functions, but in this chapter we will introduce the science of equine movement as quantified by gait analysis, and we thank our friend Russell Guire of Centaur Biomechanics for supplying the majority of the images you will see in this chapter. However, this is just a thumbnail sketch of the work that is being done in research into equine movement.

Interest into equine movement really began with the seminal work of Muybridge in 1887 which stimulated interest in the discipline with remarkable photographs of equine movement. Indeed it was Muybridge who first demonstrated using his photographs that in the gallop gait there was an actual moment of suspension when no feet were on the ground at all (Figure 7.1).

However, this brief flurry of research activity into equine movement ground swiftly to a halt when the general use of the horse was replaced by steam and motor power. The number and use of horses declined dramatically as man turned his attention to greater providers of horsepower.

A revival of interest began in the 1970s with the introduction of the concept of the sport horse and the advent of cheap computer power, and since that time the scientific discipline of equine locomotion has come of age.

For a long time expensive computerised gait analysis equipment could only be used in a laboratory setting with horses working on treadmills. Still much of the scientific work is conducted in locomotion laboratories with a

Figure 7.1 Muybridge's famous sequence of photos: The Horse in Motion.

three-dimensional system capturing up to 1000 frames of data per second which can be used for sophisticated analysis, and not generally available for commercial use with the average riding horse. Also, it is known that horses working on treadmills move differently from horses working over ground and comparisons to actual movement in athletic performance are difficult to extrapolate.

Other systems are available for general use outside the laboratory but these are only working in two dimensions so are unable to give the sophisticated data of the 3-D systems. The most easily available 2-D system used by the Centaur Biomechanics Team is the Quintic System (www.quintic. com). This bridges the gap between the laboratory-based limitations of a 3-D system as the data output is taken from a 2-D plane and mainly looks at the angular displacement of the joints. Two-dimensional analyses can also be carried out in the outdoor or competition environment therefore giving a better impression of an individual horse's movement. Indeed the Centaur Biomechanics Team were very busy taking data from horses competing in the 2012 Olympics for research purposes, and were responsible for the research behind the revolutionary Fairfax girth (see Chapter 6) which was widely acclaimed for giving Team GB Equine a competitive advantage.

For data collection, markers that can be tracked by computer are attached to the horse in standard, palpable anatomical landmarks (Photo 7.2). The camera captures up to 240 images per second, whereas the human brain can only process about 12 images per second. Computerised gait-analysis systems can, therefore, pinpoint even small errors or asymmetries in movement that could not be perceived by eye alone, thus detecting the

Photo 7.2 Standard anatomical marker placement for gait analysis.

so-called 'sub-clinical' lameness. In terms of the athletic horse, where correct dynamic and static posture are paramount, the ability of being able to pick up subtle asymmetries in movement is key to maintaining soundness and performance.

Even better, if the equine athlete has baseline movement data, against which his development can be monitored, this can be the basis for his athletic conditioning and physiotherapeutic support.

Gait analysis and movement issues

So what type of movement issues can the everyday horse rider, competitor or physiotherapist use gait analysis for, and how does it work?

As the horse moves, a video camera captures the movement of the markers applied to the horse and the system software digitises that movement so it can be analysed within minutes and displayed on a computer screen. The software effectively 'joins the dots' between the markers and displays specific segments of the horse's body. Photo 7.3 shows the segmented forelimb. One immediate visual effect is a demonstration of how the limb moves through time and space, as the markers are tracked through one stride (Photo 7.4). All markers can also be tracked by the system throughout one stride and visualised on screen (Figure 7.5).

There are obvious limitations to a 2-D system when compared with a 3-D system. Firstly, you do not get an impression of any simultaneous

Photo 7.3
Computerised image of
foreleg limb segments.

Photo 7.4 The
computer software
tracks the markers
as the horse moves,
to obtain a visual
representation of
how the limb moves
throughout one stride.
(Courtesy of www.
quintic.com)

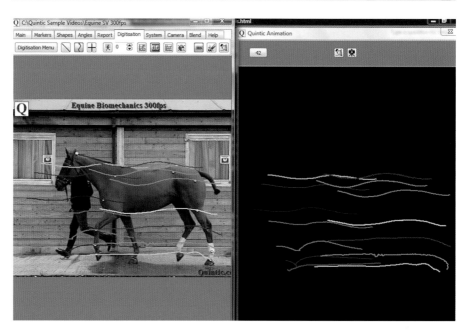

Figure 7.5 Screenshot
of marker tracking
throughout one stride.

adduction or abduction of the limb, which in terms of athletic ability can mean that you are only getting half of the picture; secondly, to make a left/right comparison, the sides of the horse need to be tracked on separate occasions, so that there is no actual simultaneous recording of both limbs. Therefore the Centaur team tends to focus mainly on measurable range of movement (ROM) of limb joints and making a comparison between left and right, but allowing for errors. For example, Figure 7.6 shows a comparison between left and right carpal (knee) movement.

There is a minimal difference in the joint angle movement between left and right in this horse, which may be down to the left and right sides being recorded at different times. However, leading the horse from different sides (to prevent the handler from coming between the camera and the horse) can also have an effect on the way the horse moves.

We are still taught that horses should only be mounted and led from the left for no better reason than that Cavalry Officers wore their swords on their left and if they mounted from the right, the sword would have got in the way of the left leg clearing the saddle.

However, this constant emphasis on always being on the left of the horse ultimately creates a subtle asymmetry. Indeed Gail commonly encounters horses that show a very slight weakness in the right hind, which can frequently be seen on the lunge on the right rein, as these horses tend to circumduct the right hind on to the midline or, in bad cases, on to the outside, and rotate the pelvis towards the centre of the circle. Gail refers to this as 'weak right hind syndrome'. Therefore it is recommended that to prevent this anomaly, you should vary the sides that you mount (and dismount) and lead.

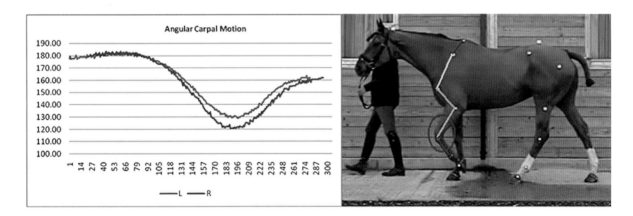

Figure 7.6 On the left is a graph demonstrating the changes in the knee joint angle of the horse walking on the right. The red trace is the right knee and the blue trace is the left knee. (Courtesy of www.quintic.com)

The hock ROM can be compared in a similar manner (Figure 7.7). When significant asymmetries are detected between left and right joints, then this would require investigation. For example, in the ROM graphs of the fetlock in Figure 7.8, you can see an asymmetrical graph of fetlock ROM which required further veterinary investigation.

Although an appreciation of subtle asymmetries in joint movement is helpful, how else can we use 2-D gait analysis in our quest for an understanding of functional anatomy? We go back to two of our basic principles of the equine athlete.

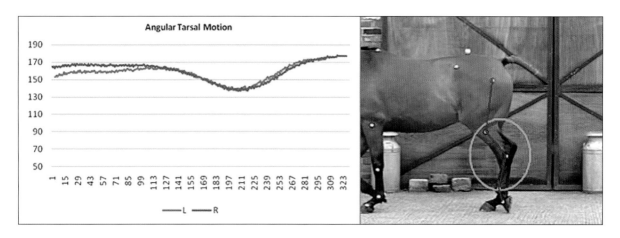

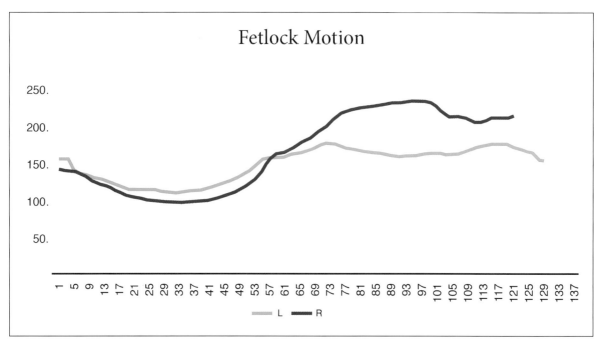

Figure 7.7 *top chart* Analysis of hock ROM. The red trace is the right hock and the blue trace is the left hock. (Courtesy of www.quintic.com)

Figure 7.8 *above* Fetlock ROM from a horse displaying asymmetrical joint movement which required further investigation.

Shoulder freedom

Freedom of shoulder movement is positively correlated with limb-stride length. We can use the gait-analysis system to measure and monitor this. In Photo 7.9 the system is being used for just this purpose.

We know from published research that a long sloping shoulder facilitates the forward and upward movement of the forelimb which in turn gives greater freedom of forelimb movement. Slope of the scapula has been correlated with higher gait scores in dressage horses.

Balance of dorsal and ventral muscular chains and lumbosacral joint movement

Again the system can make a quantitative analysis of length of hind-limb step, and how this can improve with correct schooling (Figure 7.10). The more hind-limb protraction in the cranial part of the stride, the greater the

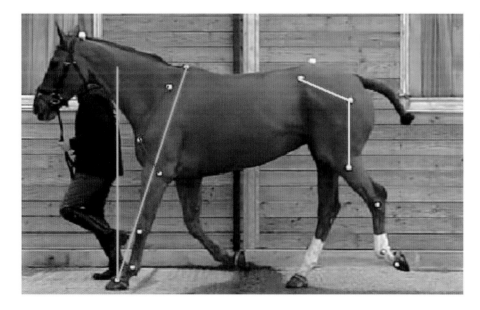

Photo 7.9 Measuring shoulder movement and step length.

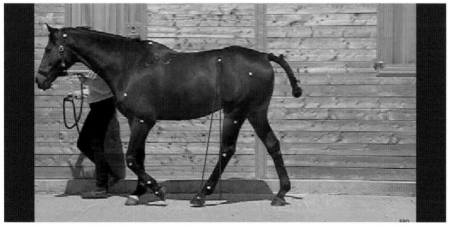

Figure 7.10 Measuring hind-limb protraction.

flexion of the lumbosacral joint in the canter, gallop and jump. However if retraction is lengthened in the caudal phase of the hind-limb stride, this would be indicative of restricted lumbosacral joint function and/or imbalance of dorsal and ventral muscular chains.

Foot balance

At this point we must mention one other issue that comes towards the top of our list for its relationship to injury, poor posture and loss of athletic function – foot balance and farriery. Again, however, we shall only be able to give a brief account of how important equine foot care is in maintenance of soundness, and we recommend that you read Gail's last book, *No Foot – No Horse: Foot Balance to Soundness and Performance*, to gain a full understanding of this important part of equine welfare.

This is not a new phenomenon, because in the third century BC the famous Greek General and horse master, Xenophon, wrote:

Just as a house would be good for nothing if it were very handsome above but lacked the proper foundations, so too a horse, even if all his other points were fine, would yet be good for nothing if he had bad feet for he could not use a single one of his fine points.

That is just as true now as it was 2400 years ago. Indeed studies carried out on the relationship of foot imbalance to lameness conclude that up to 95 per cent of all horses have some form of foot imbalance which predisposes them to injury.

Attaining good foot balance will result in a foot that is of a shape and strength to support the weight of the horse whilst providing a base for optimum movement. The foot/shoe/surface interface is the complete dynamic base from which your horse moves; after all it is (hopefully) the only part of the horse and rider that touches the ground!

As we have discussed, as a prey animal the horse's major means of defence is to run away. To propel the horse during locomotion the major locomotor muscles are sited close to the centre of mass, just as the engine in a racing car is situated close to its centre of mass. The further away from the centre of mass you get, the lighter the structures must become so that the large locomotor muscles can move the limbs through the air with as much speed as possible. There are no muscles below the knee and hock in the horse because muscles are heavy structures and would become energetically disadvantageous at the extremities of limbs. So the lower limbs are worked by a series of levers and pulleys – tendons and ligaments.

The bones in the lower limb also become lighter towards the extremities both in terms of their diameter and density, again because weight at the extremities is energetically inefficient. We can conclude therefore that the further away from the centre of mass a body part is, the lighter, less dense and more susceptible to injury it is, because there are no margins for error in the system.

If Lewis Hamilton's racing car was sent out to race with imbalanced wheels, he would probably not make it beyond the first bend. More than likely his wheels will fall off because of abnormal forces being transmitted through structures which have no margins for such error. So it is with horses. Horse movement involves a series of collisions of the feet with the ground at high velocities and unless there is near-perfect foot balance, abnormal forces are transmitted up the limbs and cause abnormal forces in other structures throughout the body. As it is the structures in the lower limb that have the least margin for error, they are primarily affected, but breakdown can occur anywhere in the body after a series of postural compensations caused by poor foot balance.

Another important consideration is elastic energy. Abnormal loading from the foot/shoe/surface interface leads to inappropriate loading of the lower leg tendons which return that energy inappropriately and cause deviations in distal limb movement. For example a horse that 'dishes', i.e. the forefoot and distal limb swing outwards during limb flight, is more likely to sustain injury. Dishing is thought to be associated with a pigeon-toed conformation and generally that is true. However, most toe-in conformation issues result not from deviations within the actual skeleton but from deviations in the hoof capsule caused by poor farriery or foot imbalance.

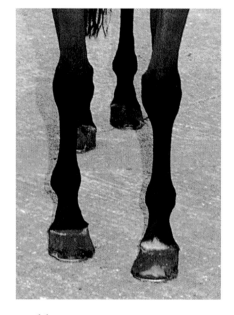

In Photo 7.11 we see a horse displaying such a toe-in conformation problem. This was a racehorse that the trainer was unable to keep sound and veterinary investigation revealed a chronic foot imbalance which was putting strain on the lower-limb tendons and creating a dynamic postural problem, resulting in lameness in the lower limbs and back pain.

So how can the average horse owner know if their pigeon-toed horse actually has a hoof capsule deformation or a genuine skeletal irregularity? To do this, simply pick up your horse's front limbs as shown in Photos 7.12 and 7.13. By dangling the legs from the knee, you can look down the unweighted limb and see if the hoof capsule genuinely hangs straight, which both do in these photos. Therefore this horse had a chronic lame-

Photo 7.11 Toe-in conformation can be caused by a skeletal malformation or a foot balance deviation and it is important to know which it is.

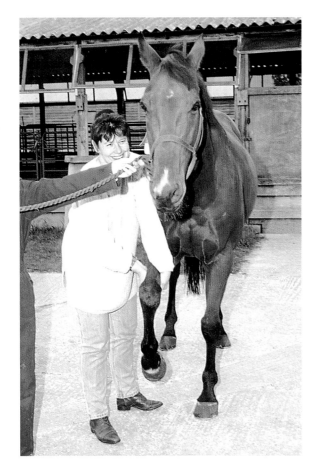

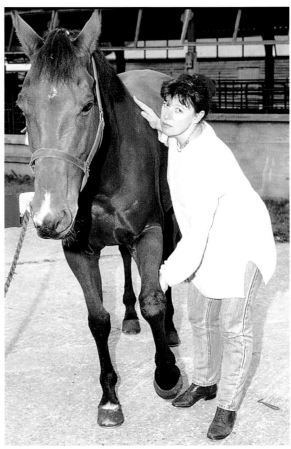

Photo 7.12 *above left* Hanging the left foot shows that actually the limb is straight.

Photo 7.13 *above right* Hanging the right foot shows that this limb is also straight.

ness problem caused by a hoof capsule deviation arising from many years of incorrect foot trimming and farriery.

Sometimes it is possible to visualise poor foot balance by eye alone, but we can also use gait analysis to ensure that a horse's foot flight is the best it can be. For example, Figures 7.14a and b show frames taken from an analysis of a moving horse by the Centaur Team; front foot on the left and hind foot on the right. The feet are just about to land on the concrete and, as is evidenced from the orientation of the front and hind feet, they are going to land on the outside of the hoof first.

This orientation of hoof landing creates abnormal forces of secondary loading in the foot created when the inside of the foot contacts the ground after the outside, which then leads to abnormal loading of the limbs. In fact if you look carefully at the front foot you can see that the inside wall of the hoof is beginning to become concave because of this abnormal foot fall.

Figure 7.15 is an illustration of what to look for in mediolateral foot balance. A perpendicular line dropped through the midpoint of the limb dissects the hoof into equal parts, with equal weight bearing on either side. Further, the slope of the quarters is equal on both sides. However, we

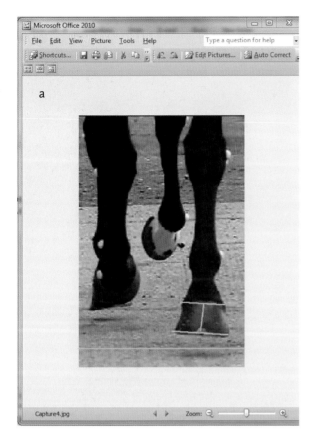

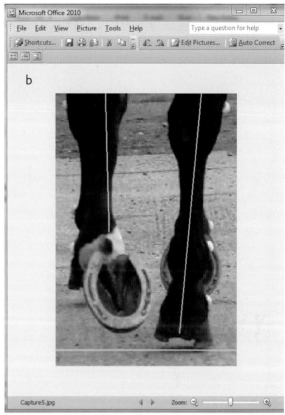

Figures 7.14a and b
above, left and right This horse is just about to land on the outside of the hoof, and not flat-footed as he should: a) front foot; b) hind foot.

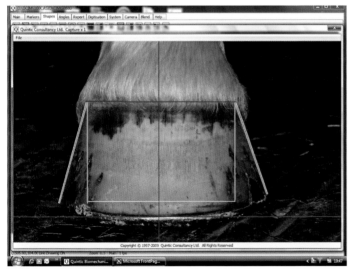

Figure 7.15 *left* Idealised image of good mediolateral foot balance.

must be careful about using this type of image as our ideal for one main reason: the coronary band is not a fixed structure and can deviate with chronic foot imbalance.

We can also look at dorsopalmar foot balance (Figure 7.16). For good balance in this plane the angles of the toe, quarters and heel should be equal. In this photograph, we can see that the heels are collapsed and

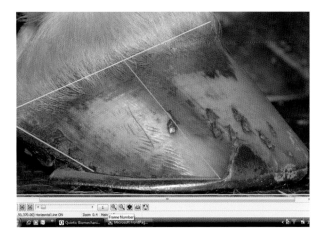

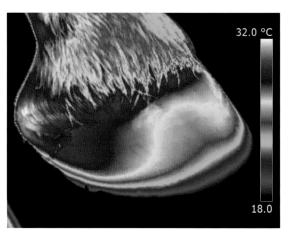

Figure 7.16 This horse's heels are collapsed and underrun. Ideally all the lines should be parallel to each other. This leaves the back of the foot lacking full support so the shoe needs to be lengthened.

Figure 7.17 Lack of heel support/collapsed heels put abnormal pressure on the back of the foot, ultimately leading to pain and lameness, as shown by the red areas.

underrun. In this case the back of the foot is left without proper support, and in this particular case the farrier has applied the shoe with extra length. If we imagine a line between the back of the coronary band and the back of the shoe, it will now be more in line. We can visualise the effect of lack of heel support with thermal imaging (Figure 7.17).

Gait analysis and static posture

We have taken a look at how we can assess movement, but gait analysis can also help us with assessing static posture and the effects of postural sway by recording any changes in joint movement whilst the horse is stationary. In Figure 7.18 we see changes in hock angles whilst the horse is standing. The problem here is that we have very little in the way of peer-reviewed scientific evidence about the posture of stationary horses and what issues affect postural sway, other than we know that hind limb neurological deficit shows evidence of increased postural sway when measured using a force plate.

We do, therefore, have much to learn about how we can scientifically quantify static and dynamic posture in the horse, and how it affects athletic ability, susceptibility to injury or the evaluation of a rehabilitation programme. We know that 75 per cent of sport horses will sustain at least one lameness event in any one season, but their long-term assessment is largely ignored – many vets feeling that if a horse is not clinically lame there

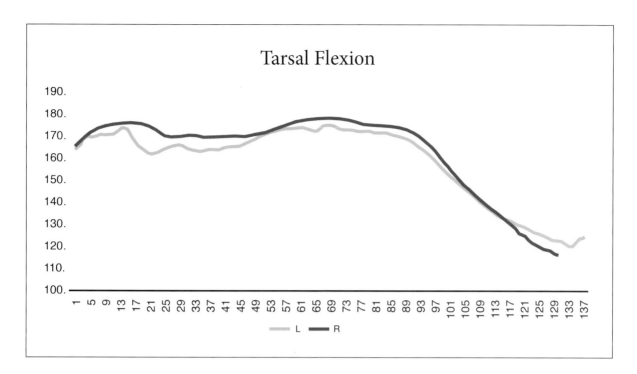

is no impedance to continued athleticism. However, postural compensations may already have been made, even though not clinically evident, and this is where the input of your ASSVAP equine sports physiotherapist is vital.

It is not sufficient to declare horses as either 'sound' or 'lame'. In the absence of trauma, these are the two ends of a very wide spectrum with a range of dysfunctional movement in between. The equine sports physiotherapist will look at your horse in terms of 'function' or 'dysfunction'.

Figure 7.18 Comparison of left (blue line) and right (red line) hock angles during standing.

CHAPTER EIGHT

The Equine Athlete:
Development, maintenance and rehabilitation

WE GRATEFULLY ACKNOWLEDGE Sam Pawley Photography for her wonderful photos used in this chapter.

Throughout this book we have emphasised the importance of shoulder movement, balance of dorsal and ventral muscular chains, and freedom of lumbosacral range of movement. In this chapter we will show you how you can achieve this with your horse. These exercises are simple to perform and involve very little in expensive equipment. Indeed, Gail has specifically designed this programme so that anyone, on any budget, can afford to build optimum foundations for their horse. You do not need a riding arena, just a few poles. However, there is no substitute for taking advice from your local ASSVAP veterinary physiotherapist and getting some individual input for your horse's particular problems.

Some of the first and most important exercises you can do involve stretching the muscles within your horse's neck, shoulder, back and hip. You will never see a human athlete competing without first having a good stretch of their muscles. Stretching muscles has many effects but the main benefits are lengthening of fibres and increasing blood flow. There still remains controversy within the sports-science literature as to whether passive or dynamic stretching is the most efficacious. Passive (static) stretching involves reaching to a point of tension within the muscle(s) and holding the stretch. Passive stretching has been used throughout the years for two main reasons: injury prevention and performance enhancement. But there is now some evidence in the human sports-science literature that passive stretching is not recommended for athletes whose sport involves quick changes of direction. Dynamic stretching involves moving parts of the body and gradually increasing reach or speed of movement, or both.

Whilst there is confusion in the human literature and little or no evidence in the equine literature as to the efficacy of stretching techniques, we will include both passive and dynamic stretching exercises within this chapter. However, Gail's experience in rehabilitating hundreds of horses leads her to believe that in a rehabilitation programme, dynamic stretching should be included in the programme, and passive stretching should be applied at the end of the exercise session. In fact this will generally apply to all horses, whatever their ability, training and athleticism.

Passive stretching

Passive stretches with your horse are generally simple to undertake as long as you remember the golden rules.

1. Ensure that the environment in which you intend to carry out the stretches is safe for both you and your horse. Particularly, do not stretch with the horse standing on concrete or any slippery surface. Always make sure that your horse is standing as square as possible.

2. Do not perform passive stretches with your horse tied up. Ask a friend to hold him for you whilst you do it.

3. Always make sure that there is enough room around the horse for you to be safe. Getting trapped in the back corner of the stable stretching a hind limb is very dangerous.

4. Once your horse has accepted passive stretches as part of his daily routine, you will find that he enjoys them, but do take care for the first few times and always make your movements slow and careful, because this will be new to him.

5. Make sure you don't injure your back, always try to keep your back straight.

6. For young horses, or those recovering from injury, hold the stretch for about 15–20 seconds. For athletic conditioning, hold for about 30–40 seconds.

7. Do not stretch further than the 'end feel', i.e. at the point where there is a resistance to your stretch.

8. If in doubt consult an ASSVAP veterinary physiotherapist.

For all these demonstrations we have used Lazy Acres Buccaneer, known as Barry at home. Barry is one of the UK's top eventing ponies and is part of the Lazy Acres Event Team, ridden by Amber Franklin. Passive and dynamic stretches form a part of Barry's daily routine, and he is an expert 'stretcher'! Don't expect your horse to be able to do these stretches as effectively as Barry straight away; these are the stretches that you are ultimately aiming for.

Shoulder and forelimb stretches

Generally individual stretches should be carried out on one limb and then the same stretch on the other limb. For example, you would do the shoulder protraction stretch on the right forelimb and then do the protraction stretch on the left forelimb. In this way you can make an assessment of any differences between the two. For example, is your horse able to stretch the left limb more easily than the right, etc? If you also make notes of your findings, you will then have a record of your horse's progress.

Protraction stretch

Pick up the forefoot, and place both hands around the back of the fetlock or pastern. Draw the limb forwards keeping the height of the hoof of the limb being stretched at about the height of the knee on the other forelimb (Photo 8.1). Hold for 15–20 seconds and then replace the foot on the ground either in line with the other forefoot or by just lowering the foot to the ground from the stretch. This will leave the foot in a position in advance of the other forefoot and will allow the horse to continue the stretch himself should he wish to.

In the photo you can see that Barry is actually leaning back slightly. As an expert stretcher, he will take the stretch to the level he wants to, and Gail can just 'anchor' the foot whilst Barry does the stretch himself.

The muscles that are being stretched here are the muscles behind the shoulder: latissimus dorsi, triceps, deltoid, deep pectorals and thoracic trapezius. However this will also stretch the limb flexor muscles.

Contraindications to any stretches are muscle damage to any of the muscles which would be stretched. Also be careful if the horse had known knee-joint problems. However, you can still do the shoulder stretch but by stretching with your hands placed behind and slightly above the knee joint.

If you want to stretch the athlete to his maximum range of movement you can raise the height at which you hold the front foot (Photo 8.2) but this is an advanced stretch so please take care.

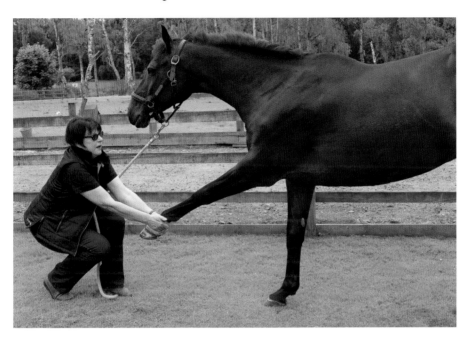

Photo 8.1 *above* Holding the protraction stretch.

Photo 8.2 *left* The athletic protraction stretch. Care must be taken with its use.

Retraction stretch

Stand at the side of the horse, facing the limb you wish to stretch. Pick up the foot supporting the pastern with one hand, and place your other hand at the front of the knee (Photo 8.3). Taking care to keep your back straight, take a step towards the rear of the horse. Using only the hand in front of the knee, draw the limb backwards until you reach the end feel. Always make sure that the limb remains level to the body and that you are not pulling it away from his side. After the appropriate time, replace the foot gently back on the ground.

This stretches the muscles of protraction, in front of the shoulder mainly: cervical trapezius, omotransversarius and superficial pectorals. The stretch can be extended to the cleidomastoideus (to gain the full brachiocephalic stretch) by the horse flexing his neck away from the limb being stretched.

Contraindications to this stretch are as for the previous stretch.

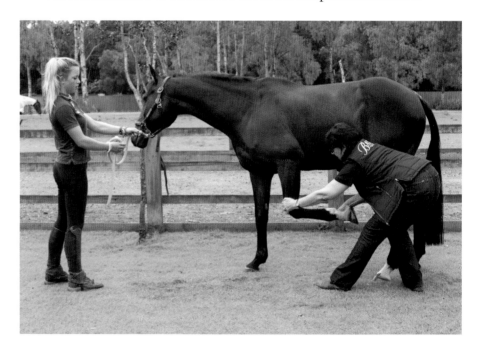

Photo 8.3 The retraction stretch. Notice that Barry has learned that by flexing his neck away from the limb being stretched, he can enhance the stretch all the way through his neck.

Abduction stretch

The abduction stretch requires the forelimb to be drawn away from the side of the body to open out the chest. Stand at the side of your horse at the level of the forelimb and facing towards it. Pick the foot up and support the fetlock with one hand whilst the other hand reaches around the flexed knee (Photo 8.4). It is very important in this stretch that you do not put any twisting pressure on the knee, so again the hand on the knee is used to

Photo 8.4 The abduction stretch to open out the chest area. Make sure that the lower leg is kept in line with the knee so there is no twisting at the knee.

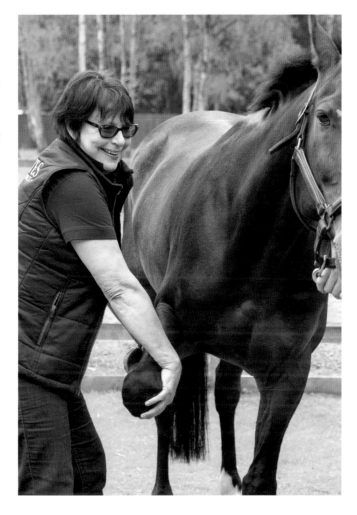

complete the stretch whilst the other hand simply supports the fetlock and keeps it in line with the knee. Once you have achieved the correct hold, lift and draw the limb out to the side. Hold the stretch for the appropriate time and then gently replace the foot on the ground.

This will stretch the transverse pectoral muscles predominantly, but will also stretch the superficial pectorals and subscapularis. However, another benefit of this stretch is that the serratus ventralis muscle on the opposite side needs to contract to stabilise the ribcage aiding balance particularly in lateral work.

Contraindications are as before.

Adduction stretch

The adduction stretch allows all the muscles which lie laterally to the shoulder to be stretched. It is also probably the one that, at first, you will have problems with because you will be asking the horse to pick up the forefoot on the other side to which you stand.

To perform this stretch stand on the opposite side of the horse to the limb you want to stretch, at about the level of the shoulder and facing the horse. Reach over and pick up the other forefoot (for the first few times you can ask a friend to help you, by standing on the other side of the horse from you, by picking up the foot and passing it to you) (Photos 8.5a and b). It is most important that you take the limb to be stretched *in front* of the limb remaining on the ground.

Once again it is important that no twisting pressure is put on the knee, so as before, just support the fetlock/pastern with one hand whilst placing the other hand around the front of the knee and, just using the hand on the knee, bring the limb across the front of the horse until to get to the end feel. After holding the stretch for the appropriate time you should then replace the foot gently on the ground.

The adduction stretch will mainly stretch the trapezius muscle, but again it has proprioceptive advantages in that it will aid balance.

Contraindications are as before.

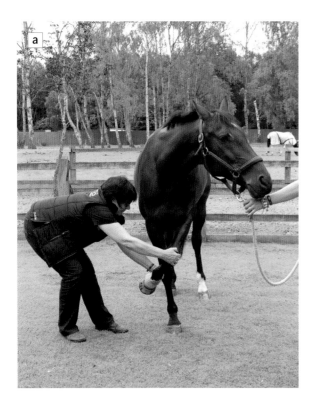 

Photos 8.5a and b The adduction stretch. You may need help from a friend when performing this stretch for the first few times until the horse understands what you are trying to do. a) It is important that you bring the leg in *front* of the leg that remains on the ground with one hand supporting the fetlock/pastern and with the other hand placed around the knee to guide the movement across. b) The placement of the leg at the end of the stretch.

Hip and hind-limb stretches

Before you consider performing any of the hind-limb stretches do please make a risk assessment. If you know your horse well and know that he will not object to you being behind him, then proceed with caution. With a horse that you are unfamiliar with proceed very slowly and with extreme caution. Again, once horses are used to stretching they find it a very pleasurable experience but even the most bomb-proof of horses can be startled by incidents happening elsewhere on the yard, so it would be good to do your stretches in a quiet part of the stables at a time when few people are about. If in any doubt whatsoever, consult an ASSVAP veterinary physiotherapist.

The contraindications to all the hind limb stretches are injury to the muscles to be stretched and hind limb joint injury, and in an injury treatment scenario stretches should only be carried out by your ASSVAP physio after veterinary diagnosis.

Protraction stretch

Walk to the hind limb you are going to stretch, whilst patting your horse along his side and down the leg so he knows where you are going. Pick the foot up and, as with the front limb protraction stretch, place both hands behind the fetlock and gently draw the limb forwards, making sure to keep the limb in line with the body and not pulling out to the side. Keep the foot close to the ground and stretch until you get to the end feel. If your horse is unused to this stretch he may snatch his foot back, so please make sure you keep your back straight (Photos 8.6a and b, see overleaf). Also make sure that you do not hold the foot too high. Think of just pointing the toe towards the heel of the front foot (Photo 8.6c, see overleaf).

This stretch is generally known as a hamstrings stretch because, as you see from the photographs, the semitendinosus, semimembranosus and biceps femoris muscles are being stretched. However, this will also stretch the gluteal muscles. This stretch is excellent for lengthening the hind-limb stride length.

Retraction stretch

Again, do make sure that you are in a safe, clear area and that you proceed with caution. Run your hand along the horse's back and down his hind leg so that he knows where you are going.

Pick up the foot and draw it out behind the horse, keeping the foot low to the ground. Whilst using one hand to support the pastern/fetlock, use the other hand to apply a downwards pressure on the point of the hock. Pressure

Photos 8.6a–c The hind limb protraction stretch. Placing your hands behind the fetlock, lift the foot (a) and draw it forwards (b). Note how straight my back is. c) Point the toe of the hind foot towards the heel of the front foot.

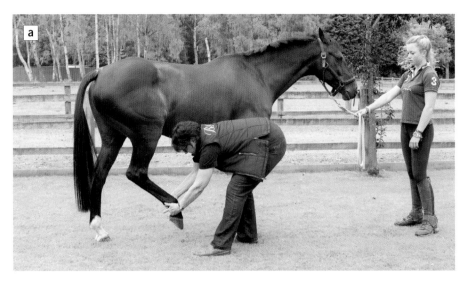

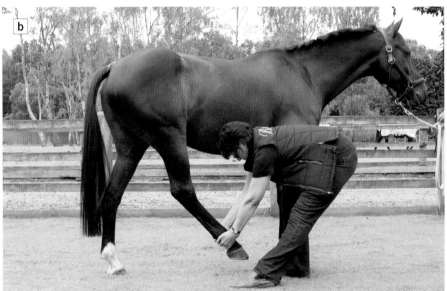

must be applied to the hock to gain the full stretch (Photos 8.7a and b). Hold for the appropriate time and then return the foot gently to the ground.

If you are in any doubt as to the safety of your standing behind the horse, this stretch can be carried out whilst standing at the side of the horse. This stretch is normally known as a 'quad stretch' in that it mainly stretches the quadriceps group of muscles, but there is also a stretch to the tensor fascia latae.

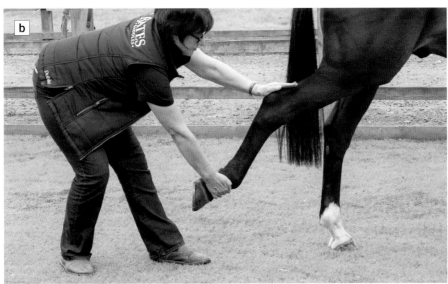

Photos 8.7a and b
The hind limb retraction stretch. Ensure that you have assessed the risk. If in any way unsure as to your safety when standing behind the horse, this stretch can be carried out standing at the side of the horse. Pick up the foot and draw it out behind the horse, keeping the foot low to the ground. Pressure must be applied to the hock to gain the full stretch.

Abduction stretch

Again, make sure that safety is paramount, both in terms of the environment and the temperament of the horse. Make sure that you run your hand along his back and down his hind leg so that he knows where you are going. When doing this stretch it is vital *not* to put any strain on the hock.

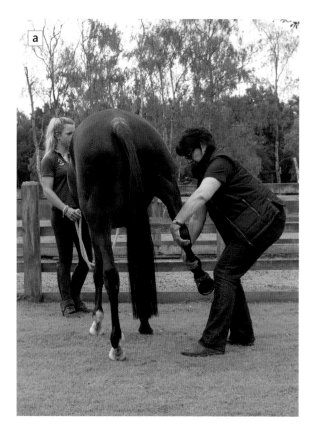

Photo 8.8a and b The hind limb abduction stretch. Care must be taken not to strain the hock as you take the limb away from the body and lift it. a) The off hind is lifted and the stretch begun. b) The leg is lifted and stretched further.

Standing level with the hind leg that you are going to stretch, pick up the hind foot and place one hand on the inside of the fetlock/pastern, with the other hand on the inside of the hock. Gently, using the hand on the hock, bring the limb away from the body and lift (Photos 8.8a and b).

Hold for the appropriate period of time and then gently lower the foot back to the ground. This will stretch all the hind-limb muscles on the inside of the hind leg such as the gracilis and the adductor.

Adduction stretch

Like the forelimb adduction stretch you will probably find this very difficult to start, but as you and your horse become more confident it will soon get easier. Stand on the opposite side of your horse to the limb you intend to stretch and bend down so that your head is level with the top of the hind limb. Reaching in front of the leg closest to you, pick up the foot of the other hind leg. Again the help of a friend can be utilised.

Once the foot is off the ground bring it across the *front* of the leg closest to you. Take hold of the outside of the hock on the leg that is off the ground as soon as you can reach it, and using the hand on the hock, draw the limb towards you, without twisting the hock, as seen in the sequence of photos (Photos 8.9a–d).

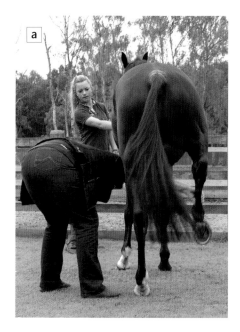

Photos 8.9a–d The hind limb adduction stretch. Make sure that you draw the leg in front of the other hind limb and do not put any twisting strain on the hock.

After the appropriate time, gently release the leg, replacing the foot on the ground. This will not only stretch the biceps femoris and the gluteals but it will help develop balance and posture.

Back stretches

These stretches are not strictly passive because you utilise basic back and pelvic nerve reflexes, but once you have learned to perform them, you will find them extremely useful for ensuring back-muscle health and suppleness.

As you will be working on the dorsal chain, it is important to stretch these muscles so that they can lengthen when the ventral chain is contracted. They also evoke movement throughout the lumbosacral joint.

These stretches can be tricky because you need to apply pressure to exact structures to achieve the reflex action and it would be wise to seek advice and instruction from your local ASSVAP veterinary physiotherapist before attempting them.

Lateral back stretches

This stretch will affect the longissimus and multifidus muscles. Keeping these muscles in good health is of paramount importance especially the multifidus which is the deep spine stabiliser.

You will need to locate the sacrosciatic ligament in the quarters, as this is where the pressure needs to be applied to invoke the reflex, but the general location is demonstrated in the photographs (Photos 8.10 and 8.11).

To perform the lateral back stretch to the left, place your left hand over the lumbar area to stabilise the lower back and with the tips of your right fingers exert a downwards pressure on the sacrosciatic ligament and then draw the pelvis towards you. This will cause the lumbosacral junction to ventroflex and lateral flex, lengthening the long muscles of the right side of the back.

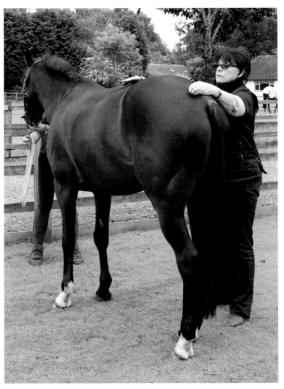

Photos 8.10 *above* The lateral stretch of the back to the left. Gail's left hand is placed in the lumbar area and the tips of her right fingers are applying pressure on the sacrosciatic ligament.

Photo 8.11 *right* The lateral stretch to the right, with the hand positions reversed.

Again do be careful because if a horse is painful in the back or lumbosacral joint he may lash out. Once you have held the stretch for the appropriate time release the pressure on the sacrosciatic ligament.

Repeat on the right side (Photo 8.11).

Spinal stretch

This involves ventroflexing the lumbosacral junction, changing the angle of the pelvis (so that the horse tucks his quarters underneath him) and stretching the long back muscles on both sides. Please take note that this can be dangerous if the horse is painful or he is taken by surprise, because you have to stand directly behind him. Although Gail demonstrates this stretch with Barry confidently, she is still in a position of danger if Barry reacts badly to the stretch. In these circumstances, you are strongly advised to perform this stretch with the horse in the stable, his quarters at the closed door, and with you outside the door.

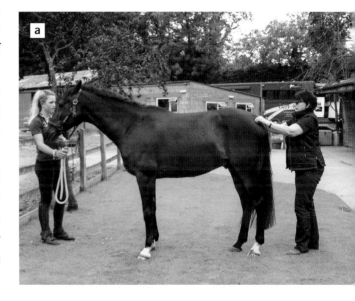

To perform this stretch you need to press your index finger and thumb together and place one hand either side of the tuber sacrale – the start position – and then slowly draw your fingers down towards the tuber ischii – the finish position (Photos 8.12 a and b).

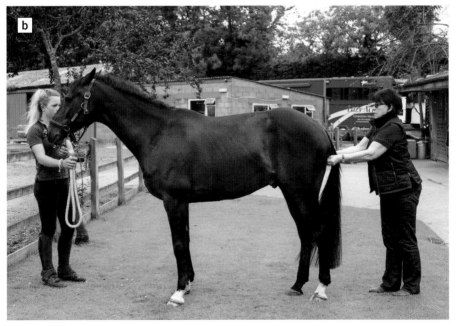

Photos 8.12a and b *above and left* Drawing your thumb and forefinger down the horse's quarters produces flexion in the lumbosacral joint stretching the long muscles of the back (look at the angle of the pelvis in the two photos in comparison with the windows of the building behind).

Neck stretches

The neck is important to maintain because there is such a lot of intervertebral movement, and it is vitally important for the athlete. Apart from anything else, you will know that any pain in your neck makes you feel miserable and affects your posture and movement. A long, supple neck helps to produce long, supple movements and improve the horse's jumping performance.

The difference between neck stretches and other stretches is that the horse needs to do them himself and will need to be tempted with a treat. That is why the stretches demonstrated in this section are called 'carrot stretches'. But they will work equally well with pieces of apple, or mints, or anything else that your horse likes.

Again Barry is a seasoned stretcher, so don't expect your horse to perform these as well right from the start but the following exercises and their photos show you what you are aiming for.

Photos 8.13a–f *below and opposite* Using a treat, tempt your horse to bring his head round in front of you as far as he can reach before allowing him to take a bite.

Lateral stretch

To get a full lateral flexion throughout the neck and open out all the intervertebral joint spaces, the easiest way is to make the horse stretch round you as demonstrated in the sequence of Photos 8.13a–f. Stand with your back against the horse's shoulder and, using the treat, tempt the horse to reach round you before you allow him to take a bite.

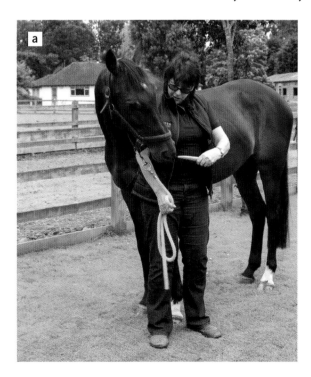
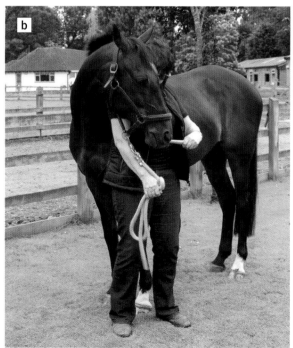

If your horse will not stretch round you, you can just tempt him to take the treat by flexing his neck along his own side rather than round you as shown in Photo 8.14. However, you can see in this photo that Barry is mainly bending round the bottom of the neck but in the previous photo sequence he had to bend throughout his entire neck.

These stretches should be performed to both sides.

Photo 8.14 Another way to achieve the lateral neck flexion is to ask the horse to stretch for the treat along his side, but this does not flex him throughout the entire neck as does the method in the previous photo sequence.

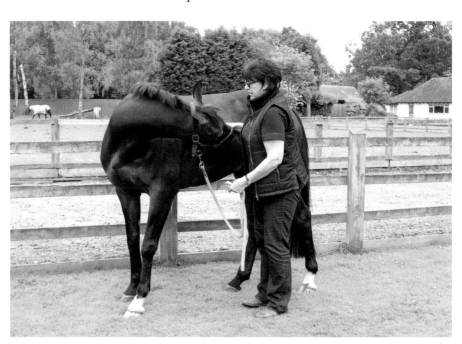

Axial stretch

It is mainly in the horse's neck that axial (rotational) movement takes place. This can be enhanced by using a stretch method that makes him rotate through the neck.

Again, using a treat, tempt your horse to take it from a point just behind his front foot. In this way he has to stretch and rotate the neck (Photos 8.15a–c).

Repeat on the other side.

Flexion stretch

This is an excellent stretch for suppling the rhomboid and rectus capitus dorsalis muscles, which very often get tight after a horse has been incorrectly schooled with the head held high. Again, this is centred on making the dorsal chain as long as possible.

Simply take the treat and tempt his head downwards to reach between his front legs at about the height of his knees (Photos 8.16a and b).

 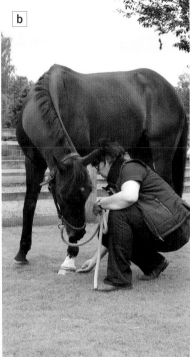 

Photos 8.15a–c The axial neck stretch. Encourage the horse to stretch his neck down and round to take the treat from a point behind his front foot.

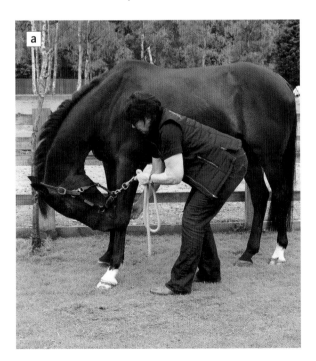 

Photos 8.16a and b The neck flexion stretch. Using the treat, bring the horse's head down and in between his knees.

Exercises in hand

A lot of people do not understand the necessity of working horses from the ground. And yet if you replaced just one of your ridden schooling sessions every week with working your horse from the ground you will reap the benefits as you get a completely different picture to the one you get when you are riding. You can watch his footfalls, are they even? Is he falling in or out? Is he tracking up? What are his transitions like? One of the most distinguishing features of good horses is the quality of their transitions. On the lunge or on long-reins you can establish transitions that you can continue working with from the saddle.

You can re-establish the balance of dorsal and ventral muscular chains by encouraging the horse to start bringing the hind leg under to work the ventral chain, the lumbosacral joint and to lengthen the neck and free the shoulder.

Passive stretching is all very well for greater shoulder, hip and dorsal-chain development, but it is also vitally important to work the ventral line and tighten up the abdominals with dynamic stretching. If you stand up and completely relax your abdominal muscles, you will feel your lower back hollow. Now if you tighten your abdominal muscles you will find that this supports your lower back. This is what human athletes call 'core stability', from which all athletic movement stems. So by lengthening the dorsal chain and tightening the ventral chain in the horse we are giving him the same core stability. However, try as she might, Gail has never been able to persuade a horse to do sit-ups and abdominal crunches! Therefore a lot of the exercises that we do in hand with horses are designed to strengthen the core. But how do we do that?

Once again, you can get the feel of what you want to achieve by trying it yourself first. Stand up and place your hands across your abdominal muscles just below your waist. Alternately lift your knees in a marching action and feel how your abdominal muscles tighten on the side where the knee is lifted. We can use this action in the horse to strengthen his core, therefore we need him to take really big steps and lift his hind limbs.

A number of people feel that working on the lunge or long reins is very difficult, and rehabilitating the seriously injured horse *is* a specialist physiotherapeutic job. But the majority of mildly dysfunctional horses can be helped by even the novice horsewoman/man if they have a structure and plan as to what they want to achieve, because most of the rehabilitation work that Gail does centres on the walk. The reason for this is that the walk is a gait in which the horse uses each leg in turn and takes it through its range of motion. The walk is a deliberate gait which acts as the foundation for movement. Once the foundations are stable then you can start to build the rest of the athlete.

Most of the following exercises can also be used when starting the young horse ensuring that they get the best possible start, and even for the elderly horse that may have some creaky joints.

Throughout this section we will be regularly referring to 'posture' and 'proprioception'. Posture is developing correct movement and core stability, for which the horse must have a full awareness of the position of parts of his body in time and space, i.e. proprioception.

Ideally you would start your exercise programme using an indoor school, and that is certainly recommended for starting youngsters, but it is not necessary and an outdoor arena or even a field will suffice. Again Gail is using Barry as her demonstration horse, so what you will see in the photographs is what you are aiming for, which is not necessarily what you will start with!

Proprioceptive wrapping techniques

It is necessary here to introduce another term: **kinesthesia**. Kinesthesia is the awareness of the position and movement of the parts of the body using sensory organs, known as proprioceptors, in joints and muscles, but it is slightly different to proprioception. Kinesthesia focuses on the body's motion or movements, while proprioception focuses more on the body's awareness of its movements and behaviours.

Kinesthesia is a key component in muscle memory, and training can improve this sense. However, equilibrium and balance is uniquely related to proprioception. We need to bring these two together in a logical and focussed schooling programme, to enable the horse to have a better awareness of movement.

One of the ways of achieving this greater awareness is to use items that you can apply to the horse's body in such a way as to provide him with the sensory feedback from the body areas that you wish him to concentrate on.

The first of these items are Ace bandages. These are highly elasticated bandages that maintain this elasticity even after washing. They are relatively inexpensive and, although not manufactured for this purpose, they are excellent for constructing all manner of kinesthesic/proprioceptive tools.

The basic wrap uses two Ace bandages to form a 'box' around the body of the horse (Photos 8.17a and b).

One bandage is tied very loosely around Barry's neck, and the second bandage is tied to the first bandage at about mid-body level, taken around the back of the stifles and tied to the same place on the opposite side. This creates a very light pressure on the back of the stifles that Barry will be aware of and it will encourage him to bring the hind limb through a little more. The first bandage will make him aware of his shoulders, and the whole wrap creates a kinesthesic loop giving feedback to his body, keeping him straight.

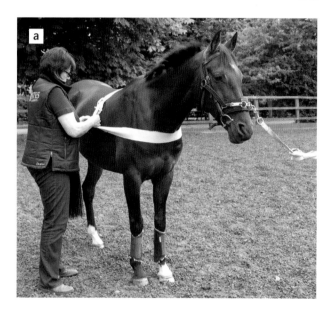 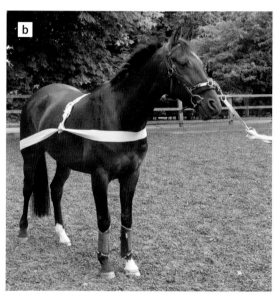

Photos 8.17a and b
Application of the basic wrap. One bandage is tied loosely around the neck and the second bandage is tied to the first and taken around the back of the stifles and tied to the other side of the first bandage.

Gail has also found that this configuration has a calming effect, particularly on young or nervous horses, so is excellent for starting youngsters. Please do, however, take care when placing the wrap behind the stifles the first few times; it can evoke a flight response. So make sure that someone else has control of the horse and they are wearing suitable protective clothing.

Gail uses long-reins and moves Barry forwards at walk (Photos 8.18a–c). (Note that the long reins are attached to the cavesson and *not* the bit; you should only attach them to the bit if you are unsure of your control.)

You can see that the stretchy Ace bandages keep contact with Barry at all times bringing continuous feedback to his central nervous system, making him aware of his body and limbs.

Just to demonstrate that this technique can be used in any situation, Photo 8.19 shows Gail using it with a 17.2hh thoroughbred racehorse that has been on box rest for nearly six months! Please note that remedial schooling in these situations is a much specialised job and you should seek the guidance of your ASSVAP veterinary physiotherapist before even attempting rehabilitation of a racehorse in these circumstances. Also in

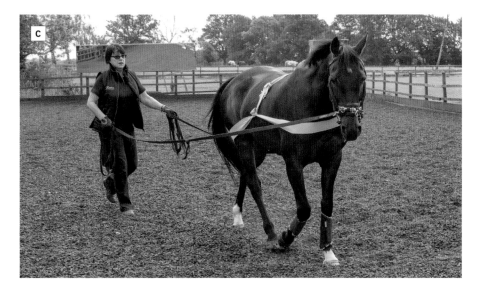

Photos 8.18a–c
Moving forwards at walk on long reins. Note the nice long hind-limb steps and straight movement.

Photo 8.19 Gail and Kerry work with a racehorse, using wraps for posture correction.

the photo is Kerry Millership who owns a rehabilitation yard. Gail works with Kerry to rehabilitate a number of horses with complex, multifactorial problems. They have a number of specialised skills enabling them to undertake this type of remedial work.

Once the horse is calm and relaxed walking forwards with the wraps applied, you can then start using different surfaces, again to stimulate proprioception and to make the horse begin to concentrate on his foot placement. For example, you could do some walking work in the school and then walk across concrete, gravel, unlevel fields, some poles etc., making sure that you perform turns and figures of eight, to keep the horse concentrating and calm.

You will note from the previous photos that the horse is not wearing a lunge/long-rein roller, and this is fine in the very early stages where you simply want to use the wrap to keep the horse straight, and you want nothing to impede shoulder movement. However, if you want to introduce circles and some more advanced exercises using long-reins, then a roller is necessary to feed the long reins through for better steering and control.

In Photos 8.20a–c Gail has applied a suitable roller and then put on the wrap that goes behind the horse's quarters. The long reins have been fed through the rings on the side of the roller. The wrap is left on the hind limbs to continue to encourage their length of step, which will also work the abdominal muscles in the ventral chain and produce greater movement in the lumbosacral junction. The long-reins are now acting to keep the shoulders straight.

Photos 8.20a–c
Gail applies a lunge/
long-rein roller and
threads the long-reins
through the rings
on the side, keeping
the wrap on the hind
limbs to lengthen step
and encourage core
stability.

Going forwards at the walk, Barry is encouraged to relax the neck, and keep his head low to lengthen the dorsal chain.

Lengthening the neck is very important in the re-establishment of dorsal and ventral muscular chains, because when the neck is lowered the nuchal ligament draws the withers forwards allowing the back to flex and lengthen the dorsal chain (Figure 8.21).

Again, when the horse is comfortable with this new arrangement, you can start to introduce more complicated remedial exercises to improve posture and core stability. One of Gail's more favoured exercises is to construct a maze, or labyrinth, of poles (Photo 8.22). This is an excellent

Figure 8.21 Lengthening the neck draws the withers forward and flexes the back.

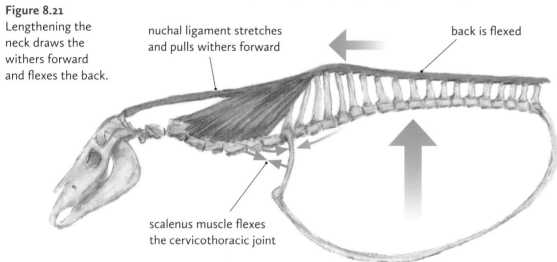

nuchal ligament stretches and pulls withers forward

back is flexed

scalenus muscle flexes the cervicothoracic joint

Photo 8.22 *below* A maze of poles on the ground. The aim of the exercise is to walk the horse through the zig-zag of the maze without him stepping outside.

exercise which requires the horse to make very tight turns in succession. In this way he has to flex through his body, abduct and adduct all his limbs and concentrate on his movement. By being behind him, Gail can appreciate any problems with the horse's movement and correct them immediately.

Just how effective this exercise is can be appreciated in the sequence of Photos 8.23a–g.

Photos 8.23a–g
Guiding the horse through the maze makes him use his legs in all planes.

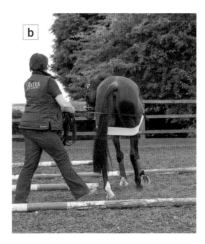
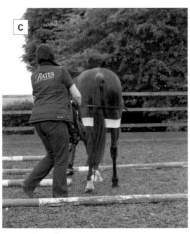

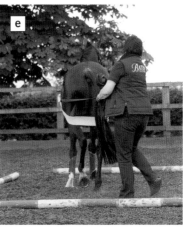

This is also a good exercise because it keeps the horse interested and concentrating on weaving through the turns. You can then come through the maze from the other direction (Photos 8.24a–e).

Once you have laid out your maze of poles, however, you can mix up the routes you take just to keep the horse interested in what he is doing. For example, you can take him over a corner as shown in the sequence in Photos 8.25a–g, see opposite. Alternatively you can use the line where all the poles of the maze line up (Photos 8.26a and b, see page 176).

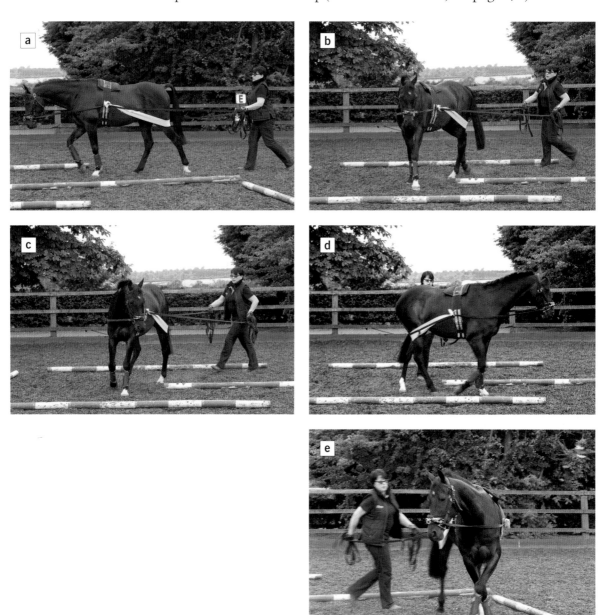

Photos 8.24a–e Working through the maze from the other direction.

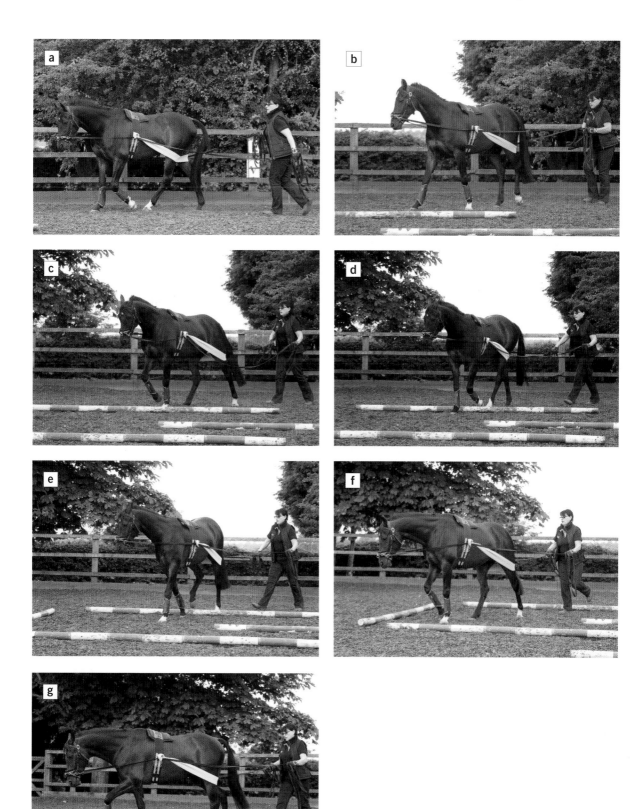

Photos 8.25a–g Adding interest to the exercise by taking the horse another route: over a corner.

Photos 8.26a and b
Walking straight along the poles within the maze.

Introducing the Pessoa training aid into your exercise programme

There are many training gadgets on the market but the one that Gail uses is the Pessoa. There have been many studies looking at the effects of the Pessoa on equine movement, most of which recommend it. However, like any gadget, if it is misused it can be extremely harmful, and many people are unsure how to use this training aid in their exercise programme.

We will briefly describe how to fit the Pessoa here and if you are applying it to your horse for the first time please take additional care. There is an excellent video on Gail's website that you can view for more information on fitting the Pessoa.

In Photo 8.27 Gail has fitted the Pessoa to Barry. Again, Barry is very used to being worked in the Pessoa and is very comfortable with it.

Once you have completed your exercise programme with the wrapping techniques, your horse should have achieved a better stride length and lumbosacral joint movement. You can then start on lengthening the dorsal chain and shortening the ventral chain by using the Pessoa training aid. Please note that if your horse has a lot of pain and muscle spasm in his back or neck, you should not use the Pessoa immediately. Use the proprioceptive wrapping technique first.

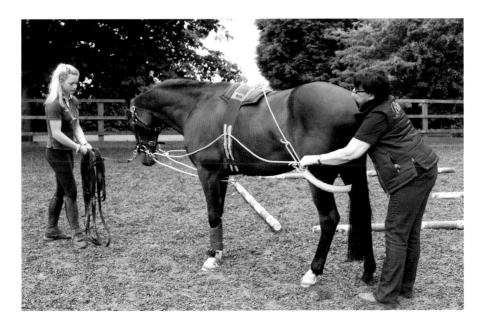

Photo 8.27 Fitting the Pessoa training aid correctly.

The benefit of using the Pessoa at this stage of your programme is that you can now start to really lengthen the dorsal chain because the Pessoa requires the horse to work with his head lower than his withers whilst continuing with the proprioceptive effect of the tensioner behind his stifles to lengthen his stride. Because of the lengthened stride, his abdominal muscles are being worked and the lumbosacral joint ROM is increased. Also, as you are lengthening the neck, you will be freeing the shoulder.

The following four points are the golden rules for effective fitting of the Pessoa.

1. Make sure that the tensioner sits just behind the stifles. You can shorten the tensioner string that goes up to the back of the roller to achieve this.

2. *Never* use the Pessoa with the lines clipped anywhere other than on the bottom of the roller. The lines are passed through the D rings on the side of the roller, the sliding clips are clipped to the bit rings, and the lines are then passed between the front legs for the fixed clips to clip on the D ring underneath the roller.

3. The tightness of the lines should be set so that when the horse works in the outline you want, the long and low outline, the lines are slack and exerting no pressure on the horse at all. Only if he works outside this outline will the lines tighten.

4. You can now fit the long reins or lunge line. Never attach these reins to the bit, you will interfere with the action of the Pessoa. Always clip

them to the cavesson. Remember: the Pessoa is clipped to the bit but the long reins or lunge rein are clipped to the rings on the cavesson (Photo 8.28).

You can now start on lengthening and flexing the neck, and you can see from Photo 8.29 how Barry is working long and low, with a lovely big stride, but the lines of the Pessoa are slack, producing self-carriage.

Begin by working through the maze once more at walk. In Photo 8.30 you can see Barry taking a tight turn in the maze, flexing through his body, in a long and low outline, crossing hind limbs and opening front limbs. In fact this photograph almost entirely epitomises the goal of any conditioning programme.

Photo 8.28 Long reins clipped to the cavesson and Pessoa lines clipped to the bit rings.

Photo 8.29 Barry works in a perfect long and low outline with long steps. This self-carriage means that the lines of the Pessoa are slack.

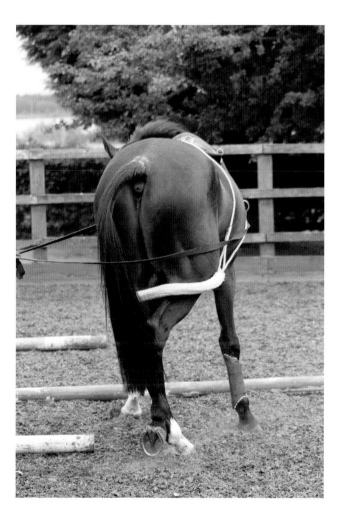

Photo 8.30 Turning tightly in the maze, long and low, flexing through the body, crossing the hind limbs and opening up the front limbs; all in perfect balance.

Bringing the horse onto a circle

We are now in a position to start bringing circles into our conditioning programme. We can also start to work at the trot (Photos 8.31a and b). Initially just work on the transitions, so a few steps in walk followed by a few steps in trot, etc. The transition should come from behind with the head remaining low. If the horse throws his head up when you ask for the transition, then keep working at the exercise until you get a correct transition. Always finish your schooling session on a positive note.

If your maze of poles is still on the ground then you can now introduce them as trotting poles (Photo 8.32).

Once your horse is balanced and moving forwards freely in self-carriage, bringing his transitions from behind without throwing his head up, you can start to work on the canter transition. Initially you might find that your horse will produce a better canter transition if you ask for it over a pole on the ground.

Photos 8.31a and b *left and below left* Still working on long reins and in the Pessoa, bring the horse onto a circle and introduce some trot work.

Photo 8.32 *below* Introducing poles into your trot work.

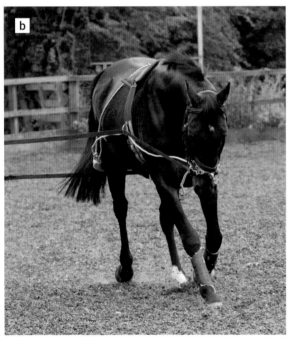

Introducing some more specialised conditioning/ rehabilitation techniques

Up to this point, the exercises Gail has described can be conducted by the vast majority of horse owners without problems. However, simply as an introduction to some more specialised techniques, which can be used for treating differing conditions, we can demonstrate some more complex techniques that should not be attempted by anyone other than a specialist in remedial exercise because anatomy and biomechanics skills are required for their correct application. Advice from your ASSVAP veterinary physiotherapist should, therefore, be sought.

Kinesthesic taping

Kinesthesic taping is a rehabilitation technique that is controversial at best. There is little evidence in the human literature as to its efficacy, let alone in horses, but some equine rehabilitation specialists use kinesthesic taping extensively to treat a number of issues. However, its correct application is a fairly complicated process, involving an extensive knowledge of anatomy and physiology.

As its name suggests, kinesthesic taping is purported to stimulate various neural feedback systems. In fact there are many claims (all unsupported by science) that they can stimulate the lymphatic system, treat kissing spines, and even correct tendon problems in foals. Use of taping is, however, certainly fashionable if not scientific.

Gail does occasionally use taping as part of a rehabilitation programme but only in conjunction with other techniques such as proprioceptive wrapping, discussed earlier in this chapter. For example, Photos 8.33a and b show Barry with a proprioceptive wrap on his head and neck, with kinesthesic taping on his abdominal muscles and across the lumbar region. The kinesthesic tape reacts like skin stretching and relaxing as the body moves, and the application of tape in these circumstances can provide a temporary proprioceptive feedback, the intention of which is to contract that portion of the ventral chain, and bring awareness to lumbosacral joint movement.

The neck wrap is to persuade Barry to lengthen and stretch his neck, with some flexion at the poll. Again this produces the long and low outline required to develop the dorsal and ventral muscular chains. However, you

Photos 8.33a and b
Kinesthesic taping together with a proprioceptive neck wrap.

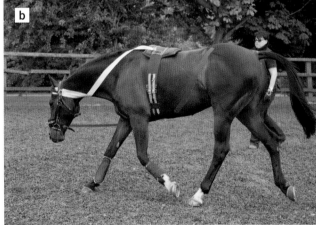

Photo 8.34 Using wraps instead of taping.

can also achieve this result using just the wraps. In Photo 8.34 a horse is being worked in a neck wrap with a stifle wrap to achieve the desired long and low outline.

Improving flexion through the neck

So far we have worked on keeping the horse stretching through his neck. However, a soft flexion through the neck, without the horse sitting on one rein or the other, is very much needed to give a nice overall picture. Again we can use the taping and wrapping techniques but introduce a novel method of lungeing with a double-ended lunge line devised by Gail. She feels that this is the best and easiest way of training horses to flex through the neck with self-carriage.

In Photo 8.35 Barry is still wearing the kinesthesic tape as before, but this time an Ace bandage has been used as a side rein on the outside.

Gail then applies a specialised lunge line which has a clip at either end (Photo 8.36). One end is clipped to the D ring at the bottom of the roller and the other end is passed between the front legs, through the bit ring, and then clipped to the ring on the front of the cavesson. The excess line is pulled through between the bit ring and the cavesson, and held by Gail.

Gail can then work Barry on a circle (Photos 8.37a and b), applying gentle contact on the bit with her right hand (Photo 8.38a) until Barry flexes his neck and immediately Gail can take the pressure off the bit and apply it to the cavesson with her left hand (Photo 8.38b). In this way the horse learns that if he flexes his neck appropriately, then his reward is the removal of the contact on the bit on the inside rein. Should he then move out of the flexed

Photo 8.35 Preparing to work on neck flexion. Kinesthesic tape is still applied, but an Ace bandage has been used as a side rein on the outside.

Photo 8.36 The application of the double-ended lunge line.

position, the contact can be re-exerted on the bit until flexion is given. At all times a contact is kept on the outside rein by the Ace bandage, preventing him from falling out through the shoulder.

Exercises under saddle

Use of kinesthesic tape and proprioceptive wrapping can be continued when you commence ridden conditioning/rehabilitation. Amber Franklin of the Lazy Acres Event Team (Barry's competition rider) can continue the exercises with Barry under saddle (Photo 8.39). She starts with similar

Photos 8.37a and b
a) Gail askes for flexion through the neck with her left hand, whilst the Ace bandage keeps a contact on the outside rein (b).

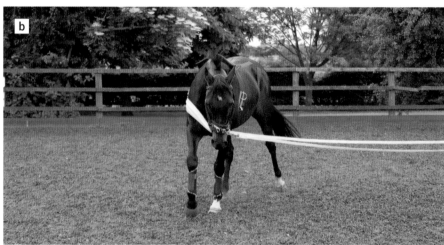

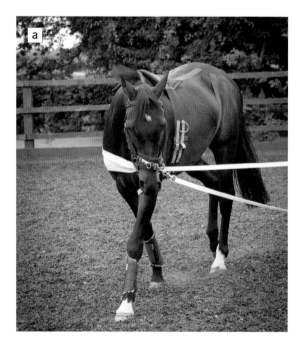

Photos 8.38a and b
a) *left* Gail takes a contact on the bit to persuade Barry to flex through the neck.
b) *opposite above* Barry has softened so Gail takes the contact on the cavesson.

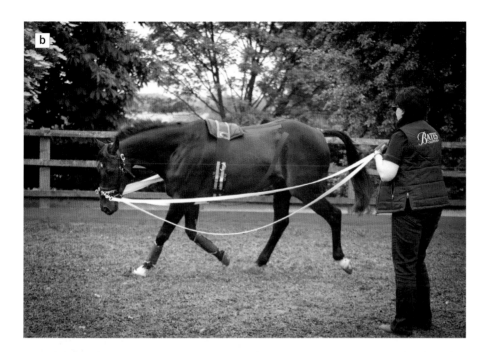

Photo 8.39 Amber rides to achieve lengthening of the dorsal chain and shortening of the ventral chain.

exercises to those completed in hand, long and low, flexed neck with the kinesthesic tape still in situ to help lift the abdomen.

Amber can now walk Barry through the maze, ensuring that she keeps the long and low outline, using a soft and open rein (Photos 8.40a–h).

You can also ride with wraps fitted. Amber walks Barry through the maze with a stifle wrap (Photos 8.41a and b).

Finally we have built firm foundations for posture and athletic performance.

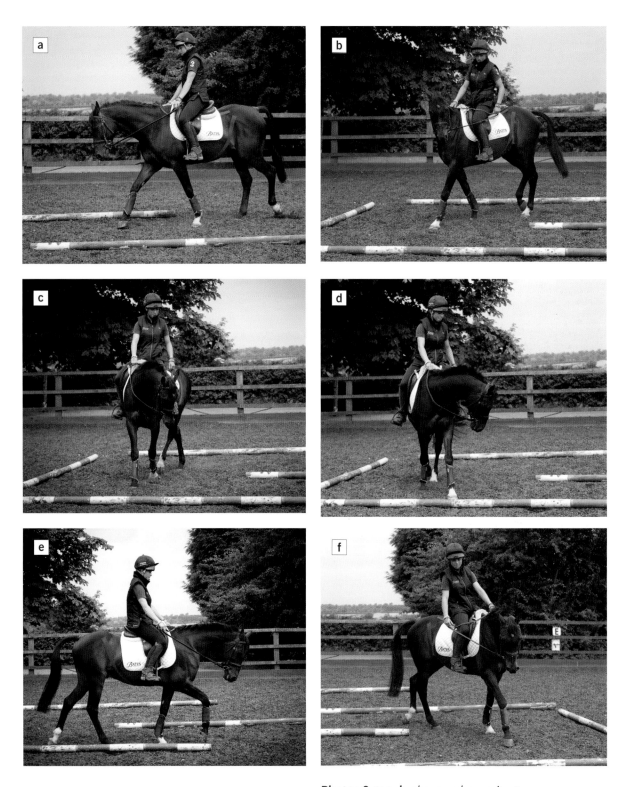

Photos 8.40a–h *above and opposite, top row*
Amber walks Barry through the maze in a
long, soft outline.

Photos 8.41a and b Riding through the maze with the stifle wrap.

Conclusion

W E HOPE THAT BY READING this book you will now feel adequately armed with all the tools for your horse to become the horse of your dreams, whether he is just a happy hacker or you have visions far above that. Even better, your horse's movement will be improved and you will have considerably lessened his chances of injury and chronic pain. After all, it is not a million miles between what Amber and Barry have been doing through the maze, to what Sarah and Skip On are doing in the Burghley dressage arena (opposite).

It must be understood, however, that this work only produces the foundations of correct movement, and to take the horse to an even higher level will require fittening work and specialist training for whichever is the discipline of your dreams. All athletes require regular physiotherapy, and just because you may feel that your horse is working well, ASSVAP veterinary physiotherapists who work regularly with equine athletes, can spot potential problems long before they become big problems. They can keep your horse working with pain-free correct posture and reduce your veterinary bills.

So whilst this book is drawing to a close, *your* work is just starting. How much effort you put in to applying your new-found appreciation of horse movement, structure, function and rehabilitation is a matter for you, but the more you do, the bigger rewards you will reap. Good luck.

opposite Sarah and Skip On in the Burghley dressage arena.

Index